The History of the Reign of Tipú Sultán, Being a Continuation of the Neshani Hyduri Written by Mir Hussein Ali Khan Kirmani

Mir Hussain Ali Khan Kirmani, William Miles

BIBLIOLIFE

THE

HISTORY OF THE REIGN

OF

TIPÚ SULTÁN,

BEING A CONTINUATION

OF

THE NESHANI HYDURI;

WRITTEN BY

MIR HUSSEIN ALI KHAN KIRMANI.

TRANSLATED

FROM AN ORIGINAL PERSIAN MANUSCRIPT,

IN THE LIBRARY OF

HER MOST GRACIOUS MAJESTY,

BY

COLONEL W. MILES,

OF THE HON. EAST INDIA COMPANY'S SERVICE.

LONDON:

PRINTED FOR THE ORIENTAL TRANSLATION FUND

OF GREAT BRITAIN AND IRELAND.

SOLD BY

Wᴹ. H. ALLEN & Co. LEADENHALL STREET;

B. DUPRAT, PARIS.

M.DCCC.LXIV.

DEDICATED

HER MOST GRACIOUS MAJESTY

THE QUEEN.

CONTENTS.

CHAPTER XX.

PREFACE.

In presenting this translation of the History of Tipú Sultán to the public, it may be proper to observe, that I do not consider myself responsible for any details contained in the work.

It will be seen that I have followed the rules I proposed to myself in the translation of the History of Hydur Alí — first, in the liberties I have considered it necessary to take with the language of the original, as to the construction of the sentences, &c. and secondly, in allowing the native historian to tell his tale without the comment of conflicting authorities, or a reference to the statements of persons, not so likely as himself to be well acquainted with the facts.

It will be evident to any one who reads this book, that although Tipú was an able man, and a brave soldier, still, that he was much inferior to his father in the characteristic qualities of a great man.

Unlike his father, he was a bigoted Mussulman, and like most of that class unprincipled and quite unscrupulous as to the means he employed to attain his ends in the propagation of his religion — with these bad qualities, his dark, suspicious, faithless character alienated those who were at first his most attached friends; and at the time Seringaputtun was taken, he appears to have had scarcely one left.

The story that he was betrayed by Mír Sádik, his Dewán, to the English, or perhaps to some of the other confederated powers besieging Seringaputtun, does not appear improbable, although unsupported by any evidence; but, as he was a great tyrant, there can be no doubt that his ministers were glad to get rid of him on any terms.

Tipú's character, cannot be better exemplified, than by the cases of Muhammad Alí, Commandant, and Gházi Khán Bede. These officers had been all their lives the most devoted and trust worthy of his father's servants, and indeed his father owed his life to them on more than one occasion, as will be seen in his history. They had been also the chief instruments of his father's elevation to the rank and power he attained, and moreover the chief means of his own accession to the throne of the Khodádád kingdom.

In return for all these meritorious services, he no sooner found himself secure in the possession of his father's authority, than he put the first to death from jealousy, because he was too just and honourable a man for the service of such a tyrant; and both were executed under circumstances of great cruelty.

It is true, Muhammad Alí, Commandant, was a violent man, that he wanted sense and entirely misunderstood his new master's character; but Ghází Khán Bede, to all appearance, was sacrificed to mere suspicion, and put out of the way only because the Sultán chose to listen to his enemies, or because he coveted the possession of his wealth.

But our sympathy is peculiarly enlisted on the part of the gallant Muhammad Alí, Commandant, when we learn from this work, that he was sacrificed to his honourable zeal in resisting the infraction of the terms of a capitulation, he, as the agent of the Sultán, had negotiated with General Mathews, at Nuggur. It is well known that the whole of the terms of that capitulation were shamefully violated by Tipú, and the unfortunate prisoners treated with the utmost brutality ; — and lastly, that General Mathews, his brother, and many officers, and soldiers were poisoned and privately murdered in prison by his orders.

It may be objected by some, that Muhammad Alí
did not resist the infraction of the capitulation in
their cases ; — from the man's character, however,
I have no doubt but that he did, though of course
ineffectually ; and I think this opinion is corrobo-
rated by the charge made against him by the Sultán, " that he was in communication and in league
with the English of Bombay, and about to seek
their protection."

By this, and other instances in these volumes,
it will be seen, that Muhammadans seldom or ever
keep faith with Idolators, (among whom they
reckon Christians,) when they consider themselves
sufficiently strong to break it with impunity. They
consider, I believe erroneously, that they have the
sanction of their religion for this diabolical prin-
ciple, but it is clear that Hydur Alí, Tipú Sultán,
the Afghan Prince at Kabul, Muhammad Akbur,
indeed, the Mussulmans in general, in all periods,
(with some rare exceptions) have acted in strict
conformity to this most villanous rule.

In reference to the spelling of the Indian names
and words in this work, I have to remark, that the
system of Sir W. Jones is followed agreeably to
the rules of the Royal Asiatic Society ; as for instance, the name of the Sultán is written Tipú,
instead of Tippoo, the old mode of writing his

name, and indeed the pronunciation of the word by Europeans.

I have not, however followed the mode adopted by some Oriental scholars in other words, as the pronunciation of the Arabic language totally rejects the infringement of one of its most common rules, ادغام under the sign تشديد.

The word Nuggur, ought perhaps to be written Nugur, but I continue the old English mode of spelling this word, because it has been so written in all works I have seen, mentioning towns of that name.

In conclusion, I trust I may be permitted to assume to myself, the merit of having made my translation as concise as possible, without any considerable deviation from the text; — and, having done this, in humble imitation of the style of my author, I beg leave to express a hope, that when my readers find errors, or inelegancies, in the language of this work, they will cast the eye of indulgence over them, and correct them with the pen of liberality and forbearance.

CHAPTER I.

The accession of the mighty Prince, high in dignity, His Highness Tipú Sultán, to the throne of Mysore, and the advance
of the armies under Generals Lang and Stuart towards Wandiwash, with other events of the year 1197, Hijri. — A. D. 1781-2.

WHEN the sun of the Nawáb Hydur's prosperity
and power, which had attained its utmost height,
shewed a disposition to decline, and the bright star
of the constellation of his Sovereignty fell from the
zenith of grandeur to the depths of disease and
death,* (in the original, affliction,) the Kháns, and
the Pillars of the State, that is to say, Muhammad
Alí, Commandant, Budruzzumán Khán, Maha Mirza
Khán, Gházi Khán, abu Muhammad Mirdah,
Purnia, Kishen Rao, &c., not relinquishing from
their grasp the administration of the current business of the government ; but, on the contrary,
taking up the ground of loyalty and obedience,
fulfilled the conditions of faith and gratitude, and
continued on the same footing all the customary
duties, usual during the life of the pardoned Na-

* وبال

B

wáb, Hydur; and, at night, after the due discharge
of the offices to the dead, the coffin containing
the body was filled with essences and perfumes,
and despatched, without the knowledge of any
other persons, to Seringaputtun; and the servants who were acquainted with these transactions
were seized, and confined separately, each without
the knowledge of the others, that they might not
be divulged.

It is proper to mention here, that at the time
the Nawáb determined to attempt the conquest
of the Carnatic Payanghaut, he also gave orders to
form, or plant, the Lal Bágh, or Garden, to the
southward of the town or suburb of Gunjam, on
this side the river Kauverí, and also to build in
that garden a Musjid, which, in the time of Tipú
Sultán, was called Musjidi A'ksá.

In front of the Musjid also, a mausoleum, covered by a dome, was erected; to superintend the
building of which a Darogha was specially appointed. At the period of Hydur's death this mausoleum was finished, and his body was therein deposited.

To be concise, the well affected. Kháns for the
present appointed Kurím Sáhib, (the brother of
Tipú) to the office of Dewán, as the Náíb of
his father; and they conducted the government

with such admirable policy, that not a particle of
sedition or disturbance occurred, either in the civil
administration of affairs, or in the army; and the
officers and men of the army remained fully assured of the perfect health and safety of the Nawáb, and with the sanction of the Dewán, and
to quiet and still the minds of the Foujdárs, and
other officers of the State, their monthly pay,
agreeably to the Hydurí regulations, was issued
to all; and the same day, one thousand horse
were detached to Nellore, and two thousand
marched towards the English camp. Still, in the
midst of all this rigid policy and secresy, the spring
and spirit of the whole army, high and low, were
changed, and depressed, as it were by inspiration,
to the gloom and darkness of mourning; and, at
times, involuntary sighs broke forth from the breasts
of both officers and soldiers.

In the mean time, however, the attached and devoted Maha Mirza Khán was appointed and despatched with letters, containing an account of the
death of Hydur, to the exalted presence of that
offspring of prosperity and honour; the tree bear-
ing the fruit of dignity and majesty, the conqueror
of the world, Tipú Sultán, who at that time
was enlightening the environs of Koimbetore
and Palghaut by his presence, and in earnestly re-

questing him immediately to direct his steps towards the camp, they made use of every expression
of solicitation and entreaty.

The Sultán on being acquainted with these
events, notwithstanding he in private received assurances from the faithful Mirza, and had his mind
set at ease by the oaths of the officers of the army,
still, was much troubled and disturbed at the appointment of Kurím Sáhib to the high office of the
Dewání ; but when this auspicious intelligence
reached the ears of his understanding, — *verses*.
" Do not listen to any one, but put thy foot in the
stirrup," — " for success and victory are hastening
to meet thee," — " a hawk cares not for a spar-
row," — " do not fear thine enemies," — " what injury can a lion receive from a lame fox." — He did
his faithful well wishers the honour to accede to
their requests, and arrived at the camp by forced
marches.

· As soon as this glorious intelligence, diffusing
joy, reached his hearty friends, the tongue of time
sang the following *verses :*[b] " Come on, for the
victorious ensigns of the King have arrived," —
" The cry of good news and victory has reached the
sun and moon," — " The resplendency of thy good

[b] It is nearly impossible to make any thing of this poetry, and
the like of it in a prose translation.

fortune has thrown off the veil from the face of vic
tory,"—" The perfectly just has arrived to redress
the complaints of the oppressed,"—" The heavens
gave promise of him to the people of the age,"—
" The time is propitious, now the King has arrived."

At once, therefore, the chiefs and officers of
the government, with Kurím Sáhib, proceeded to
meet and honour the arrival of Tipú Sultán,
and were dignified by being admitted to do homage
(kissing the ground) to that resource of the world ;
and after the customary demonstrations of mourning, at a fortunate hour, — *verses.* " Such as would
bestow blessings on the propitious signs of heaven,"
— " and make the drum of rejoicing resound to
the skies," — on a Saturday, in the commencement
of the year 1197, Hijri,[e] he was seated on the
throne of dignity and majesty, and the offerings of
felicitation on his accession were presented.

As the throne of the Mysore kingdom, from the
propitious steps of that sun of the meridian of
kingly power and authority, had risen in height
above the heavens, and as the state and its prosperity assumed the vernal splendour of youth ; in
order to reward the good services of his faithful
servants, the conquering Sultán made royal pre-

---

[e] A.D. 1783. There is no specification of the month in any
copy of this work that I have seen.

sents to every one separately; and, having honoured them by increasing their rank and pay, he
gave orders for the joyful celebration of his accession to the throne by the preparation of a feast
and banquet. — *verses*. " The King arrayed the
royal banquet," — "for that is the genial spring
and Paradise of master and servant," — " The trees
(flowers) of this garden are rubies, and the leaves,
emeralds," — "the sward or grass, glass; and the
earth, amber." — In that assembly, melodious poets
and eloquent orators, from the clouds of their invention, showered the orient pearls[d] of prose and
verse on the head of the young king, and were li-
berally rewarded from the table of his bounty.

After the conclusion of the feast and banquet,
the Sultán, placing his fortunate steps on the
throne of the regulation of the affairs of his kingdom, issued Furmáns to all the commanders of forts,
the farmers, and collectors of revenue in the kingdom ; his object being to win the affections of the
whole by his kindness and regard, and by holding
out hopes of future advancement; — from policy,
therefore, the authority every one before possessed
was still continued to them on the same footing.
About this time, the commander-in-chief of the

[d] Alluding to the Oriental mode of accounting for the formation of pearls in the shells in which they are found.

French army despatched two thousand French
troops, under the command of Count Dupleix,* to
the presence; and, after the regulation of his affairs, and finding himself fully established, the
Sultán, with his victorious army, marched to Ka-
veri Pauk, the environs of which, from the splendour of his standards, became the envy of the
starry heavens. At the same time, the English
army, under the command of Generals Stuart and
Lang, advanced to oppose the army of the Sultán by the route of Choongal Peeth ' to Wandiwash.

At hearing this news, the lion-like Sultán
marched with the whole of his army, by the route
of Doshi,' to Amloor, to repel his enemies, and encamped at the distance of about five miles from
Wandiwash; and the next day, having formed his
right and left wings, and the main body (the reserve) of his army, in order of battle, and posting
his artillery in front, he held himself in readiness
for mortal contention. The English officers, although they with their troops were drawn out in
battle array, still, seeing the order and discipline of
the Sultán's army, and the imposing appearance

* کون تپلیس
' Chingleput.
' This town is called in some MSS. Doshi Maproo, or Mamroo.

of the French battalions, did not think proper to
engage that day, but remained formed on their own
ground.

The day after that, orders were received from the
Governor of Madras, recalling the English army;
and the generals above mentioned, having destroyed the fort of Wandiwash, returned with their
display and parade to Madras. The Sultán also
marched from that place and encamped at Turva-
toor. While at this place, the Sultán's spies
brought intelligence that Iyaz Khán, the adopted
son of the late Nawáb, and who had been appointed by him to the government of the districts
of Nuggur, Gorial Bunder (Mangalore), &c., the
cup of his unworthiness being at this time filled to
the brim, had followed the path of treachery and
ingratitude, and with the greatest perfidy had delivered up the whole of the forts of that country
(Malabar) to the English of the port of Bombay;
and that unfortunate man, with a great quantity of
gold, jewels, baggage, and followers, had embarked
on board ship, and had taken his ill-starred route to
Bombay, where he had arrived; that the English
had seized the whole of that country; and that
certain seditious people, (meaning the Zemindárs,)
who had been waiting for an opportunity to rebel,
had raised the head of pride from every hole and

corner, exciting rebellion ; as, for instance, Anchi
Shamia, a Brahmun, who was at the head of the
intelligence department at the capital, (Seringaputtun,) having united in heart and hand with the
governor of the fort, planned and concerted to
effect the destruction of his master's house, and had
excited a great disturbance ; that Syud Muhammad
Khán, the son-in-law of Abdul Hulím, the Afghan
of Kirpa, also thinking this a good opportunity to
prosecute his plans, assembled a force of horse and
foot, and had made a treaty of friendship, confirmed by oaths, with the English of Mutchli-
puttun (Masulipatam), with a view to the conquest of the district of Kirpa, and was the cause of
great alarm in that quarter.

CHAPTER II.

The march of the Sultán's victorious ensigns to subdue his enemies and the recapture of Nuggur, Gorial Bundur (Manga-lore), &c. — Also the defeat of a detachment of the Bombay army, by the bravery of the Ghazies (Mussulman soldiers), and the establishment of peace between the Sultán and the English government; also the death of that brave officer, Mahummud Alí (Commandant), in the same year, that is, A. Hijri, 1197.— A. D. 1782.

WHEN the treachery of Iyaz, the encroachment of the English in that Country (Malabar), and the rebellion of the Governor of the Fort of Se-ringaputtun, &c.,—reached the ears of the Sul-tán, he, making the defeat and expulsion of the rebels his chief object, despatched Budruzzumán Khán Bukhshi with seven thousand matchlock men ; Sulábut Khán Bukshi, with six thousand Sillahdár horse ; and Mír Gholám Alí, with ten thousand irregular infantry ; all placed under the command of Mír Moinuddín, otherwise called Syud Sáhib, Sipahsalar, to defend and secure the country of the Payanghaut, while he himself with all the rest of his army and departments marched towards Nuggur.

When he had passed the Ghaut of Chungum,
the brave Muhammad Alí, commandant, with his
division of troops was sent to the capital to restore
order, to remove the disaffected, and replace them
with faithful and loyal servants ; and Kumruddín
Khán with the troops of the deceased Mír Sáhib,
(Alí Ruza Khán) was also detached towards Kirpa,
with discretional powers to oppose Syud Muhammad Khán, and the Sultán then marched by the
route of Dewun Hulli, Mudgiri and the Souba
Sura, and encamped in the environs of Chituldroog.

The Foujdár of that place, Dowlat Khán, to
manifest his loyalty and obedience attended the
Sultán with his dependants and was received with
great favour and honoured with a dress of con-
firmation on his reappointment to the Foujdárí.

When the Sultán moved on and encamped
under the Ghaut of Nuggur, Muhammad Alí, commandant, who had been despatched to the capital,
proceeded thither by forced marches by the route
of Bangalore, and encamped under the Karighat
hill, on the bank of the river.— According however to the rule, — *verse*, — [b] "O wise man fear him
who fears thee,"— " although thou mightest be able

" از ان كز تو ترسد بترس اي حكيم " [b]
" وكر با جو او صد براي بجنك "

to conquer a hundred such in battle "— and after
the fashion of wolf courtesy, began (following the
path of intimacy) to shew great regard and friendship towards the rebel governor of the capital, and
sent a message to him to the effect, that if permission were accorded, he would enter the Fort
alone and sleep one night at his house, that he
might have the pleasure of seeing his family and
children, and that the next morning, according to
the orders of the Sultán, he would proceed by
the route of Koorg to the attack of Nuggur.

The Killadár lent a willing ear to the deceiv-
ing words of the commandant, and gave orders to
the guards of the fort that he should be admitted;
and he seeing all things favourable to his views
and hopes, at night held his detachment in readiness, and crossing the river placed his men in
ambush near the walls of the fort, and gave them
orders that when he should enter the fort, and
his Turee or trumpet sound the charge, they
were immediately to enter and man the walls,
bastions and gates. Accordingly he, accompanied
by fifty brave and experienced men as a guard,
immediately after entered the gate of the fort and
sounded his trumpet, and having seized and bound
the guard, posted his own men at the gate. In
the meantime at the sound of the trumpet, the

troops in ambush swiftly advanced from their con-
cealment, and entered the fort and extended their
guards and sentinels on all sides.

The brave commandant now quickly advanced
to the houses of the Killadár, and his deputies, and
to that of Anchi Shamia and his colleagues, and
before they could open their eyes from the sleep
of neglect and folly, they were dragged out of
their beds and put in prison. — The next morning,
with the sanction of the Sultán's mother, some of
the rebels were blown from a gun ; the companions
of Shamia impaled, and he himself loaded with
irons and confined in an iron cage — a fit punishment for his villainy.

The office of governor of the capital was now
transferred to Syud Muhammad Khán Mehdivi, a
friend of the Sultán's, and the defence of the
city was entrusted to the care and responsibility of
Assud Khán, Risaldár, a brave and very able man
and who was also an old servant. — Muhammad
Alí having effected this, immediately marched with
his troops by long stages, taking with him the
letters of the Sultán's mother, and his report of
the arrangements made at the capital, and arrived
in camp at Nuggur, and detailed all the circumstances to the presence.

The Sultán was well pleased with his services

and presented him with a gorget and a Khillat or dress of honor.

The next day the Sultán ordered the passage of the Ghaut; and his troops with the greatest gallantry quitting the roads of the mountain, where detachments of the English with guns and musketry were posted, ascended by a route on the opposite side in the rear of the enemy, and commenced firing on them.

The parties of the English before mentioned now to save themselves from béing cut off, assembled in one place, and bravely fought their way into the fort.[1] — The brave and faithful troops of the Sultán now immediately surrounded the fort, raised batteries against it, and used their best endeavours to batter down its walls. It happened however one day during this period, that a stone which was thrown from a mortar into the fort, fell on a part of the wall, under which was a well full of water ; and breaking down the wall filled up the well with its rubbish. From this cause a scarcity of water arose in the fort, and the want of water carried away the strength and constancy of the hearts of the garrison.

One night, therefore, near one thousand musketeers with two or three thousand pioneers and

[1] The siege of Nuggur.

inhabitants of the place with brass and earthen
vessels came forth from the fort, and taking as
much water as they could bear away from a tank
near the walls, carried it into the fort. The Sultán being informed of this, the next night stationed guns, musketry and rifle men on the
mounds, or banks of the tank, and when on that
night they came as before, rolling on like a dark
cloud full of rain, the lightning and thunder of
the guns and musketry, drowned some in the sea
of their own blood, and some washing the hands
of their presumption with the water of despair, and
breaking the vessels of their good fortune with the
stone of flight, sought the protection of the fort ;
but notwithstanding this extraordinary state of
things, the thirsty garrison held out for two days ;
but at length the officer commanding in the fort,
through the medium of the brave Muhammad Alí,
proposed conditions of surrender, and gave up the
fort to the servants of the Sultán, and was placed
under the protection of his government, — thus by
the aid of the Sultán's good fortune, this fort was
taken in eighteen days, and some person present
on the occasion gave the date impromptu in the
following words, حیدر نگر گرفته [k] or 1197 Hijri.[1]

From this place the Sultán proceeded without

[k] Hydur Nuggur taken.   [1] A. D. 1782.

delay towards Gorial Bunder (Mangalore), and
on the road fell in with and surrounded a body
of English troops, which under the command of
Colonel Campbell, was advancing to the relief of
Nuggur ; with supplies of all kinds.

The horse of the Paigah being encouraged by
the promise of free plunder, and the Kuzzaks and
Silahdárs stimulated by the promise of one hundred rupees for every horse killed in action, were
ordered to attack this force and destroy it. It
happened that in the field, where this action was
fought, there were two tanks, or ponds of water,
at a distance of about a mile and a half from each
other.

According to orders, therefore, the Risalas of
musketeers and irregular foot (brave as lions), the
rocketeers and artillery were posted on the road
to these tanks, and they kept up a continual fire on
their enemies.

The Kakur and Chapao horse [m] were sent to
throw the enemy's baggage and followers into confusion, while the Sultán with a select few and his
body-guard, made desultory charges and attacks

[m] A parenthesis in the original. —
Although these are included in the Bede tribe, they carry off
the palm even from them in the arts of robbery and oppression,
and are the most notorious thieves in the world ; for with their
bamboo spears, they will risk their lives for a sugar cane.

on the main body. The Colonel above mentioned, however, kept the ground with great constancy and valour until mid-day, when at length his ammunition failing, by degrees the order and courage of his force, which consisted of four thousand (native) infantry, twelve hundred Europeans and seven guns was broken, and a terrible shock and great disgrace fell on them and they were destroyed.

Hussein Alí Khán the Bukshi of the Paigah (or body guard), the brother of Assad Alí Khán, the chief of Bhikanpilly, at the commencement of the action had given up two guns to the English, and after losing most of his best men was obliged to retreat.

The Sultán being much grieved at this loss, told him, if he had any of the honour or courage of a gentleman left in him, to recover the guns. To retrieve his honour and character, therefore, he with seven hundred men lightly equipped, advanced and fought so energetically against the English, that he was the chief cause of their defeat and destruction :— at length having received eleven musket and bayonet wounds he left the field grievously wounded, but victorious.

But to return,— The Sultán having taken possession of all the warlike stores and equipment of the defeated army, presented to his own brave sol-

diers ; armlets, gorgets and strings of pearls, and
then without the least delay, marched on and at
one assault took the Pettah, or suburb of the fort
before mentioned (Mangalore), and directed the
commencement of the siege and conquest of the
fort : in a very short time, therefore, notwithstanding it was the depth of the monsoon, and
that the rain fell in torrents, so that a man could
not put his head out of his tent, or his feet on the
ground : and that casts or models of animals might
have been taken from the impressions of those
dead lying in the mud ; heavy batteries were
thrown up, approaches pushed on, and a continual fire of guns, musketry and rockets maintained, and some vessels being seized, the passage to supplies by sea was blocked up. The
besieged also, who were well known for their
hardihood and constancy in braving the labours
and hardships of war, crowded the walls and bastions of the fort and for three months defended
themselves valiantly.ª At last, however, from the
length of the siege and the want of provisions, they
were reduced to great distress, and they then sent
a messenger to the presence to ask for quarter,

ª The First Grenadier Battalion of the Bombay army formed
part of the garrison at Mangalore on this occasion, and gained
great honour by its gallantry during the siege.

and they were received under the protection of the Sultán.

Every one, therefore, according to his merits received a respectable command in his service, and the foreheads of their attachment were made resplendent by the symbols of faithful service. (From this it appears, that those who joined the Sultán were Hindoos.) — Mangalore, Hoonawar, &c., having been taken by the victorious Sultán, he determined to return to Mysore by the route of Koorg and Bul. It happened by a melancholy fatality, that in the course of this journey, the brave Muhammad Alí, commandant, for a trifling fault, and for shewing too much obstinacy and presumption threw away his life. The detail of this event is as follows, that a certain Kásim Alí,* governor of the fort of Nuggur, a servant of the late Nawáb, and who, during the government of Iyaz Khán, had charge of that fort, had colleagued with that traitor, and followed the path of perfidy and rebellion ; and when the English troops arrived from Bombay,

---

* It appears from this, that Muhammad Alí, commandant, lost his life for insisting that the terms of the capitulation made by General Matthews at Nuggur, should be observed in the case of Kásim Alí, he, being the agent employed in its negotiation. It is well known that it was most shamefully violated by Típú and that both the General and his brother, with many other officers and men were barbarously murdered by that tyrant's orders.

gave up the fort to them without resistance ; he
accepting the post of Lieutenant-governor:—When
the fort however was recaptured, he, seeing the
road of safety shut against him, sought the protection of the brave commandant before mentioned, and having taken from him assurances for
the security of his life and property, took up his
residence in his tent. The Sultán, therefore, one
day inflamed with anger, sent for this Governor of
the fort to the presence, and when he arrived addressed him to the following effect ;—that the fort
of Nuggur being full of provisions, the means
of defence and a good garrison, how was it possible it should fall into the hands of the enemy ?
That allowing a mean, ungrateful slave had traitor-
ously rebelled, he (Kásim) who was a man of
good family and appointed to the charge of this
strong fort, what did he do, that for only one
day he did not perform his duty as governor, and
try to resist and repel his enemies.

He in reply said that, although there were abundance of stores and provisions, still, the Náíkwars
(Hindu chiefs apparently), and the chiefs of districts
at the suggestion of the traitor, Iyaz, acted contrary
to his, Kásim's wishes ; and having made a secret
agreement with the enemy, without his knowledge,
admitted them into the fort ; that he, the Sul-

·tán's slave, being without remedy, determined to
proceed to the presence, but that his enemies
prevented him. The Sultán then said to him,
—" allowing the truth of what you state, why
were you not prepared against the arts of the
Náíkwars, or Náírs, and why did you not send intelligence of this to the presence; and besides,
when you thought your best policy, present and
future, lay in the surrender of the fort, why did
you allow the money and property of the state to
be gratuitously plundered by the enemy, and why
did you not take as much care of it as you did of
your own?" that in this matter he was undoubtedly
an ungrateful faithless servant; — to conclude, the
Sultán having established his guilt, by the advice
of his council of state the delinquent was sen-
tenced to be impaled. The next day Zein al Abidín the Bukhshi of the Kutcheri of regular infantry (the son of Assad Khán, Mehkurri; Foujdár of Kishingiri), received orders to put the
sentence in effect, and other officers of horse and
foot were attached to the Bukshi above mentioned
to be present at its execution. The Bukshi, troops
&c., having assembled at the place appointed, they
sent for the prisoner who was under a guard of
the commandants, when he himself accompanying the prisoner came to the place of execu-

tion and said, this man has claimed my protection,[p] you must forgive his offence, or you must first put me to death and then execute him.

The Bukshi and the rest of the officers reported this in detail to the presence, and the Sultán said we will spare the criminal this day for the sake of Muhammad Alí, but let him be placed under our own guards and this therefore was immediately done.

The Sultán now sent for Muhammad Alí in private, and repeated his determination to execute the prisoner, and told him that his opposition in such a measure tended to disturb and interrupt the operations of government, the regulation of the different departments of the state, and to do away with the example necessary to be shewn to others —that he, the Sultán, in punishing this man only acted as directed by the provisions of the divine law, in order that other governors of districts and towns of the kingdom, might in future avoid the commission of such crimes : but, that leaving that alone, punishment was indispensable in a newly established government ; that the controul and regulation of the troops and country might be ensured, for that it was a saying of the wise " in order to confirm or establish your

[p] In virtue of the capitulation and surrender of the fort of Nuggur apparently.

government you must give the sword no rest."—
But, notwithstanding the Sultán for two hours
expostulated with him, and advised him not to
oppose the execution of a convicted malefactor,
still he, with his original obstinacy, which indeed
belonged to his nature, and because his last day
had arrived and the hand of death was striking the
drum of his departure on his shoulders, paid no attention to the commands of the Sultán, but rose up
and went away without asking leave,—*verse*—" advice makes no impression on crooked minds, or obstinate men"—"the branch of the stag's head is not
made green by the rain."—The Sultán was much
displeased at his disrespectful conduct, but, on account of former acquaintance and services, took
no notice of his insolence, and remained silent that
day. The next day the fire of the Sultán's wrath
flamed violently, and he again gave the same orders to the Bukhshees as before;—but when they
took the prisoner to the place of execution, the
idiot before mentioned from excess of folly or presumption, not knowing that *(verse)*—"to seek an
opinion contrary to that of a king (tyrant), is to
wash your hands in your own blood." Arrived on
an elephant and taking the prisoner from that fatal
place, and mounting him on his elephant called
out,—" any one who will join and support me let

him follow us ; " — two or three hundred musketeers of his own Risala therefore joined him, and
altogether they took the road to Seringaputtun.
As soon as this had taken place, certain persons
who were his enemies, and who, during the whole
of his life, had been seeking opportunities to effect
his destruction, represented this circumstance to
the Sultán, the reverse of what was intended, as
that Muhammad Alí had rebelliously taken the
criminal and was proceeding to the port of Cochin,
and there was no doubt but from that place he
would proceed to Bombay, and that in such circumstances to allow him to remain alive, was in fact
to give up the whole of his kingdom and authority.

Hearing this story, the Sultán despatched horse
and foot to trace his steps, while he himself,
troubled and agitated, mounted his horse and followed them ; and Syud Humíd, an officer from
Arkat, a man of great stature, and strength, and of
great abilities, was sent on in advance with Gházi
Khán to compel him to return. These two officers,
therefore, with a large body of troops pressed on
and overtook and surrounded him on a hill, about
four Kose from the encampment of the victorious
army ; and with soft words and threats brought
him round to the right path.

As the foolish fugitive was now ashamed of his

conduct, he dismounted from his elephant and stood alone, when the Sipahdár, or commander before mentioned, laid hold on his hands and he with the criminal doomed to death, and the soldiers who had followed them, were presented by him to the Sultán, who without any delay ordered Kásim to be impaled and the commandant to be heavily ironed and placed in a covered palankin and des-patched to Seringaputtun.

The Sultán after this returned to his tent, and to punish the contumacy of the men who had followed the commandant, some were put to death, and some after having their hands and noses cut off were turned out of the camp. These poor men, who had been punished for their companion-ship with the prisoner in irons, followed him for two stages, crying out to him, " Oh thou vile in-cendiary, thou art the cause of our ruin; our hands and noses have been sacrificed to our sense-less love of thee."

When these cries reached the ears of the com-mandant, his feelings of honour and compassion were violently affected, but he repressed his agi-tation as best he could until night, and at mid-night having performed his ablutionary duties he cut out his tongue, or rather drew it out by the root; and like a lamp at the approach of morning, died. Some say that he had a diamond ring on his finger, and that having taken out the diamond and rubbed it on a stone, he swallowed it and so died.[q] Some one found the date of his death in the following words رکن دولت بانتاد The prop or pillar of the state is fallen, 1198 Hijri.

When the people of his escort the next morning found him dead in the palankin, they took him up and returned with him and his horses to the presence, and all the furniture and moveables of his house were one by one examined by the Sultán. Among the articles was a small box, locked, and on its being opened and examined, several letters from English officers were found, written and sent to him during the expedition to the Payanghaut to induce him to join them, and promising him in that event large Jageers, &c., which letters, although that faithful servant had answered by scornfully rejecting their offers, still, from his extreme simplicity he had neglected to tear up, — these, by accident passed under the angry inspection of the Sultán and when therefore the contents were explained, they became, or were made, the grounds of obloquy and reproach, and the suspicion which had been

[q] Colonel Marriott's copy says his grateful master assisted him in his departure for the next world, by the administration of a dose of poison.

entertained of his disaffection and treachery was confirmed.

The Sultán, therefore, gave orders that the commandant's corpse should be dragged outside the camp and there left, and his sons were made the Sultán's slaves, and his Khadima or wife, was given as a wife to one of his (the Sultán's) slaves, a worthy and excellent man, who kept her in respectability and honour to her death, and never addressed her by any other name than mother, and indeed treated her in every respect as if he had been her son.

The mother of the Sultán on hearing of these events, which arose entirely from misunderstanding, was much grieved, and cursed the hasty anger of her son, and sent for his, the commandant's, widow who resided at Seringaputtun to live with her in the Hurum Sera, or Seraglio.

The deceased commandant, although a man of blood, and very intemperate, still, was universally known for his liberality and generous support of the poor, and monthly and yearly forty or fifty Fakírs, or religious mendicants, spread their carpets in his tents, and resided there, and often elephants, palankins and horses presented to him by the Nawáb, were given away by him in charity to these men to that extent, that the deceased

Nawáb, knowing his liberality, frequently repurchased them from them, and when occasion required bestowed them again in presents on the commandant. The fame of his generosity to the poor extended so far, that whenever a party of these religious beggars assembled at the gate of the palace, calling out for charity, Hydur Alí was accustomed to send word to them to go to that low or vulgar fellow, (meaning the commandant), and he, pleased beyond measure at the compliment, gave up to them whatever he had of money, plate, utensils, clothes, &c.

After his death, when his property was examined, in his own chest, they found nothing but some old clothes, a religious mendicant's cap, and a coat, or frock presented to him by Amin Sáhib a Mushaik'h of Arkat, who was his Moorshud, or spiritual guide, and forty cash or copper coins with the impression of an elephant upon them. But to return : — After these events, the Sultán having consigned the charge of the forts of that quarter to the most faithful and distinguished men among his servants ; Budruzzumán Khán, who left the force of Syud Sáhib after the battle of Cuddalore,ʳ which circumstance will be mentioned here-

ʳ Some words left out in all the MSS. here ; but this appears the meaning as they stand.

after, was now summoned by the Sultán, and appointed to the Foujdári and government of the district of Nuggur, and the Sultán then marched towards Koorg, when at this period arrived Mr. Sadleir, Colonel Dallas &c., on the part of the governor of the port of Madras, in order to renew and confirm the relations of peace,* and, with expressions of friendship and regard, they presented rich dresses, and a profusion of gold and jewels, to the servants of the Sultán ; and with well weighed words or explanations cleared away the dust of enmity from the mind of the Sultán : after therefore the preliminary arrangement of the conditions of peace, and amity, and the accomplishment of their objects, they with Abdul Wahab Khán, (who had been a prisoner in Seringaputtun), and certain European prisoners returned to Madras.

The governors of the forts and districts in the territories of each of the opposing nations were now recalled.

The Sultán's mind being now set at ease by the establishment of peace, he determined to revisit his capital, and he therefore marched and encamped with all his retinue and army in the vicinity of the Bul district, and having named that fort Munzirabád, he gave it in charge to a brave

درصدد *

officer as governor, and selected and appointed
Zein al Abidín Mehdivi, who was a favourite
servant, to the entire government of Koorg ; and
gave him strict orders to displace, imprison, and
punish all the rebellious and seditious people of
that district ; and the capital of that Souba, which
was before called Murkera, was named Zuffurabád.'
The Sultán after this dismissed him, and about
the conclusion of the year, at a fortunate hour entered his capital Seringaputtun.   On this occasion
the chiefs and nobility, such as the Sadaut and
religious chiefs, according to custom, went out of
the city to meet him, and had the honour to kiss
the victorious stirrup, they being also received with
distinguished marks of favour.

When the kingly throne became enlightened by
the resplendent countenance of that sun of the fir-
mament of victory, (the Sultán), he addressed himself seriously to the regulation of the country, his
army and all the departments depending on his
state, and revised and altered the rules and prin-
ciples of the protection and defence of his kingdom
after a new form ; — for instance, in former days,
that is in the time of the deceased Nawáb, the
exercises and manœuvres of the regular troops were
arranged and performed, and the word given ac-

' The abode of victory.

cording to the French system of military evolu-
tion or tactics,— but, now, the Sultán drawing
the pen of examination or correction through that
system, with the advice of Zein al Abidín Shus-
tree, (the brother of Abúl Kasím Khán, Hydura-
badi, who was also honoured with the title of Mír
Alum Shusteri), he changed the military code of
regulations and altered the technical terms or words
of command, above mentioned, (the French), to
words of the Persian and Turkish languages ; and a
separate treatise called Futtah al Mujáhidín ᵘ was
written by Zein al Abidín and his system was confirmed. From the regular infantry, five thousand
men being selected, they were named a Kushoon,
and the officer commanding that body was called a
Sipahdár. In each Kushoon were four Risaladárs
or colonels of infantry, and one of cavalry, and
under the orders of each Risaladár or colonel,were
ten Jowkdárs or captains, and on that scale or
proportion one hundred men being a Jowk, the
chief of them was called a Jowkdár, every Jowk
or company included two Sur Kheil, ten Jema-
dárs, and ten Duffadárs. — In the regiments of
· troop or regular horse,ˣ which were formed and

فتح المجاهدین ᵘ

ˣ Teepdár, equivalent to Risaladár, and Teep Risala, according
to Kirkpatrick.

appointed after the manner of the Europeans, the
Teepdár and Soubadár who, in the French and
English languages are called major and adjutant,
were called Youzdár and Nakíb. In distinction
to the Nakíb of the Kushoon and Ṙisala, he, who
was called Yussakchi,[7] had his name changed to
Shurbushum. The officer commanding three or
four Teeps, (regiments of cavalry), was called Mokubdár. In this mode he invented new terms in
all departments, as will be succinctly mentioned
hereafter.

The Shoostri before mentioned was now appointed to command the Kushoon of the deceased
commandant, and after some time he was known
to every body by the sobriquet or nick name, of
" Chup gír Dumuk[*] "—" shoulder, or carry
arms."

About this time the Bar or regular infantry,
Kutcheri, was called the Jysh Kutcheri;[*] the troop
or regular horse Kutcheri, the Uskeri Kutcheri ;
and the Bundeh, or Slave Kutcheri, was called the
A'sad illáhi Kutcheri.

---

[7] Adjutant or Brigade major, there is much confusion in this
detail in all the copies.

[*] جـب کـیر دمـک

[*] The Kutcheri consisted of from five to six Kushoons or Brigades. The word originally appears to have been applied to a
hall of audience.

CHAPTER III.

An account of the operations of Mír Moinuddín, otherwise
called Syud Sáhib, the Sipahsalar of the Sultán in the Payanghaut
province, and a description of the battles fought between the
Syud, the French, and the English troops, and his return to the
presence; also, the conclusion of peace in the same year, that is
to say, the year 1197 Hijri, or A. D. 1782.

WHEN the Sultán marched towards Nuggur, Syud
Sáhib, with his own division of troops, was encamped on the Walpundul river, and while there,
spies brought intelligence, that Colonel Lang with
his force had proceeded suddenly by forced
marches from Trichinopoly, with the intention of
taking possession of Kurroor and Dindigul.

The moment the Syud received this information,
he despatched Budruzzumán Khán, with all the
musketeers and artillery in advance, to oppose
him, while he himself followed after him with the
rest of his troops. When, however, the above
mentioned Khán had arrived at Turwur Palah,
Osmán Khán Turín, the Governor of the fort of
Kurroor, notwithstanding he had a very strong
garrison, and abundance of warlike stores, resign-

ing his courage and confidence, gave up the fort to
the above mentioned Colonel, and he himself went
and joined Roshan Khán and Sriput Rao, who had
been appointed to reduce the rebellious Naimars.
The Colonel, in the mean time, leaving a garrison
in this fort, marched on and laid siege to the small
fort of Arawa Koorchi, and was using his best endeavours to take it, when the Khán abovementioned
arrived in his neighbourhood, and encamped on this
side the Amravuti river.[b] The Colonel, as soon as
he was aware of the arrival of the victorious army,
left his batteries and encamped on the opposite bank
of the said river. The next day, however, seeing
the small number of the Sultán's troops, he gave up
the idea of attacking them, and recommenced the
siege of the fort; repaired his batteries, and renewed his fire on the walls. The Khán, therefore,
having consulted his Risaldárs, selected a certain
Jowkdár, named Kumruddín, and his Jowk or company, completely armed, and appointed him Killadár, or Governor; and despatched him at night
to the fort under the escort of the Risala of Him-
mut Khán Bukhturi, (the nephew of Payinda
Khán,) and the Risala of Bubur Alí Beg, with or
ders to attack the enemy. As soon as these Risaldárs received their orders, they advanced with the

[b] The Mysore side, apparently.

greatest bravery, and attacking the advanced or outlying pickets of the British troops in flank, and dispersing them, they escorted the Jowkdár and his company to the fort, and then returned. The Colonel, the next morning, finding a reinforcement had reached the fort, in the greatest rage imaginable, ordered his artillery and musketeers to fire at a particular part of the fort, from the morning until mid-day; at which time, the wall on one face being levelled with the ground, his troops made an assault.

The garrison, notwithstanding they bravely exerted themselves to beat back the storming party, and for two or three hours handled their arms manfully; still, as the hand of death was striking the drum of their defeat and destruction behind them, they all lost their lives.

The English troops victorious, therefore, after taking possession of the fort, turned their faces towards the attack of the Khán's camp; the Jowkdár, however, who has been before mentioned, having crept out by a water drain, escaped and joined that force. The Khán, now finding his troops unable to cope with, or oppose the English army, retired by a night march to the vicinity of Dharapoor.

Roshan Khán, however, and the before mentioned Rao, remained hovering round the English

army, making Kuzzak, or desultory attacks, when
Syud Sáhib arrived,[c] and after a period of five or
six days, and the treachery of Osmán Khán Turín, the Killadár of Kurroor, being established, he
was impaled. The troops were now formed to
attack the English army, when a letter from Monsieur Bussy, the commander-in-chief of the French
army, arrived, stating that the whole of the English army had advanced to the vicinity of Kuddalore, to give battle ; and that the Khán, with his
force, was to return, and after the defeat of their
proud enemy, they would together proceed to make
all necessary arrangements in the quarter in which
he then was. Syud Sáhib, therefore, immediately
on receipt of this letter, appointed his two Dusta-
dárs, (colonels or generals of cavalry),[d] to remain behind, giving them strict orders that to the utmost
of their ability, they should prevent the soldiers of
the enemy from plundering the peasantry and inhabitants of that quarter ; and he himself marched
by the route of Tatingar Putti, to Totum Moosli,
and there halted one day, when his spies brought
him intelligence that a great quantity of stores and

[c] This relates to the former passage regarding Syud Sáhib.
[d] A Dusta is, or was formerly, a body of twelve thousand
horse ; latterly, however, the term was applied to a much smaller
number by Típú.

provisions belonging to the English army, were deposited in the fort of Kurtullum, and that it was guarded by a few foot soldiers only.

The Khán, therefore, accompanied by the Risalas of infantry alone, marched and commenced the siege of this fort : — it happened however that the site of the fort was surrounded by the running streams of the river Kauverí, and the irrigated fields near it were deep mud and covered with green crops. The garrison, which consisted of not more than twenty or thirty men, withstood gallantly the multitude of their assailants, and prevented their effecting an entrance, and indeed exerted themselves with such energy in the repulse of their enemies, that the Syud after attacking and fighting the whole day returned at night to his encampment, and appointed a number of Kuzzaks to watch the fort, for this reason, that the next morning he intended to attack with artillery and to carry ladders with him, and after taking the fort to put the English garrison to the sword, in revenge for the loss of his men slain in the fort of Arawa Koorchi.

The garrison, however, not thinking themselves safe, the same night taking what articles they could with them, and burning the rest, marched off to Trichinopoly, which was distant about five fur-

sungs, or nearly eighteen miles. The Syud, therefore, now marched from that place and proceeded
to Kuddalore by the route of Durwachul, or War-
dachul, and the Khán before mentioned, with the
artillery and Risalas, was despatched to the fort
(of Kuddalore), to the aid of M. Bussy, while he
himself (the Syud) with the remaining horse and
foot marched towards Selimbur.*

But to return :— The English army under the
command of General Stuart, by forced marches,
arrived by the route of Pondicheri, and Bagore,
and encamped on the river Koorth, on the western
side of the fort of Kuddalore.

The French at this time kept five hundred men
with twelve guns, equipped after the manner of
the English, in readiness as an advanced picket,[f]
and the Hyduri Risalas agreeably to the orders of
the Khán, were posted on the right of the French
and strengthened their position there by raising
batteries for their support. After a period of
three days the English General, during the night,
took possession of a hill in front of these bodies of
French and Mysorians, posted guns on it, and
made all ready to open his fire, when very early

---

* Called Chillumbrum by the English.

[f] منتلاي signifies the forehead in Turkish, — also an advance guard.

next morning, the commander of a ship which had
arrived from Madras, fired three shots at the fort,
and the men in the batteries left them to see the
ship * and what she was about to do ; — at this period the fire of the guns from the hill suddenly
opened one after another.   The English regiments,
(European), marched to attack those of the French,
and the battalions of Sipahees also marched to
attack Hydur's Risalas, and had arrived very near ;
— In this situation of affairs the French being
formed, retired towards the fort leaving their guns ;
and the Mysore Risalas, not having time to withdraw their guns, and not waiting until they received orders from their commanding officer,
turned their faces towards the sea and took to
flight.

A certain Bahadúr Khán Risaldár and Bubur
Alí Beg, however, with the greatest gallantry and
presence of mind, retired facing the enemy, taking
with them the guns of their own Risalas, and
brought them to the ditch or glacis of the fort, and
there halted.

The English troops, therefore, took the batteries
and remained conquerors.   In these circumstances
the commander-in-chief of the French troops assembled fifteen hundred Frenchmen, without ar-

* The sight.

tillery, and placed them under the command of Monsieur Dupleix and Colonel Ambeau, (perhaps Rochambeau) to repel the English : — As soon, therefore, as the French troops received their orders, they in excellent order, their arms carried and their line well formed, marched, and stepping out boldly entered the field of battle.

The English European troops, who amounted in all to three or four thousand men, with their ranks closed, by a sharp cannonade killed a great many of the French, but the French officers without flinching, advanced close to their enemies and poured into their ranks a most destructive fire, and for one Pher, or more than two hours, the battle raged unremittingly, for as soon as the brave fellows had done what they could with their fire, they rushed on and engaged hand to hand, and shoulder to shoulder with their bayonets. On both sides, therefore, such a furious struggle ensued, that at seeing it, the hearts of the clouds of heaven became water, and from the concussion of the fierce charges of these iron men the earth shook to its centre.

Time, that tyrant, hard hearted as he is, at seeing the killed in this hard fought battle, shed showers of tears, and Behrám (Mars), the blood drinker, from fear at the blood shed by these valorous men, fled to the fifth blue fortress of the skies, (the fifth heaven). For two hours, therefore, during this mortal strife, those present in the battle, saw and heard nothing but the smoke and thunder of the guns and musketry; but at length the English European troops lost all power to keep their ground, and they, therefore, retreated.

At this conjuncture, the Karnatic battalions, (the Madras native regiments) [h] formed up quickly from the right and left, and covered the backs of the European soldiers [i] with their own bodies, and gained the day, for they most gallantly drove the French before them. The French troops, therefore, of whom only five or six hundred remained, retreated and gained the fort. At this time one thousand Frenchmen, who in daring pride and intrepidity carried their heads to the skies, formed and advanced from the fort to repel their adversaries, when at this critical moment, the English troops retired to their ground of encampment, and the battle was left for the decision of the next day.

The French troops halted and bivouacked at about the distance of an arrow shot from the fort.

[h] The translator regrets much that he has no means of ascertaining the numbers of the Madras native regiments, who thus nobly distinguished themselves.

[i] The Colonel of one of the retiring regiments is said to have expressed his surprize at the unsteadiness of his men, they being as he said all *tried* men, that is, men tried at the Old Bailey.

After two or three days, during which the English were marking out or raising batteries, and the
French were occupied in endeavours to frustrate
their plans, a treaty of peace which had been
made between the French and English governments in Europe, arrived ; — the two armies, the
French and English, now, therefore, became one,
and all enmity and contention ceased. The officers of both armies met and ate, and drank wine
with each other at the same table. At the same
time, therefore, by the mediation of the French
and with the consent of Muhammad Alí Khán,
Suráj ud Dowla, a treaty of peace and friendship
was established between the Sultán and the English.

But to return : — Budruzzumán Khán, and Syud
Sáhib, having effected a junction, marched towards
Turwadi, but after the conclusion of peace, with
the permission of the Commander-in-chief of the
French army, they proceeded onwards and encamped near Beelpoor. After halting there a
month, they again marched and encamped on the
river Walpundul, on account of the abundance of
forage there to be obtained. One day however,
while halting at this place, a storm suddenly a-
rose at an unseasonable period, and fell with great
violence on the Hyduri camp, and the river
swelling at the same time carried away and de-

stroyed the property of the merchants and poor
people of the camp, and many men and women
were carried by the force of the stream to the sea
and drowned. Most also of the merchants and ar-
tizans of the camp were reduced to poverty—the
camp, therefore, was immediately changed, and the
troops marched and encamped to the northward
of Arnee. At this place a Risaldár named Hurri
Singh was assassinated by his own soldiers in some
dispute regarding their pay, and from this place
also Budruzzumán Khán proceeded to the presence.

During this period Muhammad Moraud, the
civil governor of Rai Vellore, after having collected
about sixty or seventy horse, and two or three
hundred foot, made excursions on the country
surrounding, to the distance of six or seven Kose
(ten or eleven miles), and exacted supplies of provisions from the Hyduri and Sultáni districts,
(those of Mysore) and extending the hand of devastation, frequently set fire to the houses and
habitations of the poor inhabitants, and reduced
them and the produce of their fields and gardens
to ashes. It happened one day that he made a
forced march by the route of Kiriatum, with the
intention to attack the fort of Sautgurh, and at
night having by great exertions climbed up one side

of the mountain, to the top, arrived at the gate of
the fort. It happened at that time that the wife
of a foot soldier of the garrison, being about to
cook her morning meal, was standing on the wall
pouring out the water in which she had washed
her rice, and seeing the ranks of the assailants advancing, set up cries of " they are come," —
" they are come, " and immediately threw the
vessel containing the rice, on their heads. The
sleeping garrison at this, awakening and spring-
ing up from their slothful slumbers, immediately
seized their arms and with the bow, musket,
rifle and rocket, steadily opposed the storming
party, so effectually indeed, that the governor before mentioned being foiled, was obliged to take
to flight, and arrived a fugitive at Belinjpoor; —
but as there happened to be a picket or outpost of
the troops of Shah Moraud Risaldár, (the military
commandant of that quarter), stationed in a temple of the town, they immediately attacked him,
and he was obliged to retire from thence also, but
not until he had plundered the town and taken
much spoil. He however halted for a short time in
the river Belinjpoor,[k] when the Risaldár above mentioned, who was stationed near Amboor Gurh
hearing the vollies of musketry immediately got

[k] Written in some copies Berinjpoor.

his men ready, and following the footsteps of the officer before mentioned, (Muhammad Moraud), rapidly advanced, overtook and surrounded him in the bed of the river, and in one vigorous attack put the whole of his soldiers to the sword, taking all the property they had plundered to his own charge and keeping.

The unlucky Muhammad Moraud, therefore, with only fifteen or twenty horse, returned and entered his fort, (Rai Vellore).

At this time an order from the presence was issued directing that the country of the Payan-ghaut should be delivered up to the English, also detailing the terms of the treaty of peace, and re-calling Syud Sáhib. In obedience to this Firmán, therefore, all the governors of forts, collectors of revenue, &c., of parts of that country, (the Payan-ghaut), were recalled, and some of the strong hill forts with the fortress of Alumpunah of the Souba of Arkat, which had been restored and repaired, were again dismantled and broken down, and the Syud with all his troops and followers having crossed the Ghaut of Chungum, arrived at Tripatoor, and from that by the route of Hoolidroog and Pung-loor joined the Sultán ; at this period the address and ability manifested by Mír Sadik in the intelli-gence department, during his official duties as

Kotwal of Arkat, and of the army ; — having well pleased the Sultán, he was at once raised to the dignity of Sáhib Dewán, (Prime Minister). At this period also, ambassadors arrived at the presence, with letters and presents of great value from the chiefs of Poona, and the Nizám of Hydurabád, containing congratulations on the Sultán's accession to the throne, and (the former) requiring him to send the horse shoe[1] tribute in arrears for two years, and these persons having discharged their commissions, they demanded the Chouth or fourth of his revenue.

At this demand, the world conquering Sultán, being exceedingly excited, addressed the embassador to the following effect ; — " Do you not know that our deceased father, may his sins be forgiven, spent all the money laid up in his treasury, with the revenue of his kingdom for three years in the expedition or war of the Payanghaut,[m] and that by the advice, and at the instigation of your governments (the Mahrattas and Nizám) having exerted himself faithfully and nobly in conquering that country, he stepped from the throne of this world to that of the next ? — that with all this exertion, you, notwithstanding your engagements,

نعل بهاي [1]

[m] Coast of Coromandel.

to assist him, gave him no aid whatever, as by
your treaties you were bound to have done.

" Nevertheless, by the favour and blessing of the
Almighty, and by the fortune of our victorious
arms, in all this time we have not been compelled
to seek the indulgence or favour of any one, little or
great : — for the mighty and true giver of victory
made us conquerors in every battle.— After the
death also of Alí Hezrat (Hydur), the traitor Iyáz,
the slave of our house, who had risen to great
honour by the kingly benefits and favours he had received, — *Verse*, — " Too much kindness from a
master is the enemy of a servant." — " Excessive
rain is as bad as lightning to the crops or harvest."
— From the impurity of his wicked disposition determined to destroy the foundations of the prosperity of his patron and master as quickly as he could,
and his head being filled with the vapours of pride,
from his possession of money, jewels, rank and dignity, he gave up all the towns, villages and forts
in his charge to the English. Notwithstanding
this, by the blessing of God, with very little labour
that country has been all reconquered by us and
the troops of the enemy destroyed. This is well
known to the world at large. You will, therefore,
tell your masters that at present we have no treasury (money), that we should pay the horse-shoe

tribute, but that we have a number of guns and
muskets inherited from our pardoned father (Haz-
rutí Marhoom) and they are ready at their service.
However, after the settlement and regulation of
this country, orders will be given to the treasurers
of the Khodádád to send the customary amount pay-
able to you." After this address to the ambassadors, containing rules and instructions, for their
guidance; from motives of policy and precaution,
he despatched a certain Muhammad Osmán, a
servant of the late Nawáb, a discreet person well
acquainted with the forms of courtesy and the
etiquette of society, to Poona, with money and valuables, and certain curiosities from the country of
the English, plundered by his troops in the province
of the Karnatic, merely as a lesson or warning.

CHAPTER IV.

The marriage of Boorhanuddín, the most worthy of the sons of Lalamean (who was the brother-in-law of the Sultán, and slain at the battle of Churkooli), with the daughter of Budruzzumán Khán, the Foujdár of Nuggur, and his appointment and Mission to conquer the Hill Fort of Nurgoonda — also the insubordinate conduct of the Chief of Punganoor, and the appointment of certain kushoons, or brigades, to punish and reduce him to subjection — also the repair of the Fort of Ruhmaun Gurh. — Occurrences of the year 1198, Hijri. — A.D. 1783.

AFTER the Sultán had arrived at his capital, and had completed his arrangements for the regulation of his army and kingdom, his enlightened mind determined on the celebration of the nuptials of Boorhanuddín Khán, and by the counsel and advice of his ministers and chief officers, he selected the lady of the Serai of nobility and virtue, the virgin daughter of Budruzzumán Khán, Nayut, Soubadár of the district of Nuggur — a man whose loyalty was well known to, and appreciated by the Sultán ; and the Khán was therefore summoned from his government at Nuggur. When therefore the Khán arrived at the foot of the throne, he was honoured with princely gifts, and apprised

E

of the views and intentions of the Sultán, and the
Khán seeing opposition to his commands would
involve his detriment and disgrace, and notwithstanding his wife and children were averse to the
marriage, he determined to agree to the Sultán's
proposition. The officers consequently who had
the charge of preparing the banquet, and on whom
devolved the responsibility of the royal feasts,
according to the orders received by them, arrayed
the joyful banquet, and in a very short time by
the performance of the established customs of felicitation and invitation, obtained the approbation
of the Sultán; at that time the spies and news-
writers on the banks of the Tungbhudra river,
wrote to the Sultán, that most of the tributaries
of the kingdom of Mysore were disaffected and
ready to break out in open rebellion, and that
they had put forth the hand of violence from the
sleeve of rancour and infidelity, and that their
cruelty and oppression had caused great misery,
to the whole of the Sultán's subjects ; and not
only that, but from the vice of their dispositions
they intended ulterior mischief, as for instance,
Kalia Desye, that is, the chief of Nurgoonda had
opened the doors of fraud and treachery on the
peasantry of the country, and the sighs and complaints of the poor and afflicted had ascended to

the heavens — that he, day by day advanced his foot
beyond the limit of his ability, and like the Punganoor Poligar, moved by the devil, had lighted up
the fire of revolt and rebellion — that he had neglected to discharge the Paishkush or tribute due to
the Sultán for two years, and had most insolently
attacked the Fort of Sudum, a dependency of the
Sirkar of Kurum Goonda, and had plundered the
towns belonging to that fort ; — that he had several
times attacked the said fort, and had made many of
the officers or dependents of the Sultán drink the
cup of martyrdom, — also that the Poligar of Muddun Pulli had joined him heart and hand, and
was also the cause of great tumult and disturbance.

At hearing this news, the fire of the Sultán's
wrath flamed high, and considering the safety and
comfort of his subjects as inseparable from his
honour and responsibility, he immediately dispatched Syud Ghuffar, the Sipahdár with his
Kushoon or brigade to Nurgoonda, to ascertain
the state of affairs there ; the Sipahdár therefore
marched, and having after many stages arrived
there, soon obtained a perfect knowledge of
the whole affair. It appeared certain that this
man (the Chief of Nurgoonda) devoted to villany,
was instigated and aided in his rebellion by Pu-

rusram the Chief of Mirch, whose son was betrothed to his daughter, and that being vain and
conceited at this connexion, he had raised his
head to the clouds and was possessed with the
vain desire to be the ruler of the districts, lying
between the rivers Kishna and Tungbhudra, and
hearing of the arrival of the Sultán's troops, from
the natural malignity of his disposition took the
path of ingratitude, and advanced to oppose them.
The Sipahdár above mentioned on discovering his
intention, and while he was selecting a secure position for his troops, wrote to the Sultán acquainting
him with these circumstances.

Boorhanuddín, the Sipahsalar, therefore, with
five thousand horse and three Kushoons, the Sipahdárs of which were Syud Humíd Shaíkh
Oonsur, and Ahmud Beg, was appointed and
marched to take the fort, and make the rebellious
chief a prisoner, — Shaíkh Omr the Sipahdár, also
with a Kushoon, two thousand irregular foot, (Ahshám) and six guns was appointed to root out the
Poligars of Punganoor and Muddun Pulli.

When the said Shaíkh Omr marching by Pan-
gloor, and Dewun Hulli, arrived near the mountainous district of Gywar, which lies to the eastward of Nundi Droog, and encamped there, he
heard from some of the chief landholders and

53

government guards of the roads and passes,[P] that
among these mountains was one very high and on
its summit a wide plain, that it possessed a fountain
or reservoir of water, the depth of which could not
be fathomed, by the line of science, that on this
mountain was the foundation of walls built with
stone, and that they appeared to have been in
old time a fort, but long since in ruins — that if
the walls were rebuilt, they would afford a strong
defence and refuge to the Sultán's troops, and that
a force stationed here would undoubtedly ensure
the obedience of the country in the neighbourhood.
The Sipahdár, therefore, with some of his officers
and those who made this statement went up the
mountain, and examined the place and much admired it, and then wrote a description of the mountain, and the representations of the friendly people
of that district to the presence. He then marched
on, and encamped in the neighbourhood of Punganoor, and notwithstanding he strove to advise
and guide the chief, he still rebelliously advanced to
oppose him, and with twelve thousand foot occupied the posts on his route, ready for action. In
consequence, in the neighbourhood of Rama Sumoodram, a town on his frontier, a very sanguinary

[P] منیوار Persons who receive a stipulated allowance for the
care and protection of the roads and mountain passes.

battle was fought between the two parties. The troops of the Sultán, however, like lightning daily burned up the harvest of the infidel array, and with the bayonet, musket, and the keen sword, gashed the heads and breasts of their misguided opponents.

At length the brave Sipahdár in one attack with his sword cut down the commander of the enemy's troops, and immediately separated his head from his body; and the infidels seeing this, lost the footing of stability and confidence, and turned their faces to flight, and they made the Hill Fort of Bhooi Koonda, which is surrounded by a dense and impe netrable forest, their place of refuge.

The Sultán's troops having plundered and destroyed all in their way, and taking the fort of Rama Sumoodram at one assault, marched towards the said Koonda, and after the labours of five days that fort was also taken from the enemy, and the Sipahdár and his Kushoon obtained great honour, and having thus defeated the Infidels at all points they marched on. The Poligar of Punganoor whose name was Shunk'h Rayel or Rawul, ⁴ hearing of the defeat of his troops, and being in great trepidation, gave up the fort of Punganoor to his con-

---

⁴ The ancient Kuchwasa Rajpoot Chiefs of the eastern part of Gujarat, the brothers or relations of the Rana of Chitore, or rather Oodipoor, were called Rawul.

fidential servants, and sought refuge on the top of the mountain of Awul Pilly, four kose distant from the above town, and surrounded by a fearfully thick forest, where he collected together three or four thousand brave foot soldiers.

When the Sipahdár had defeated the Infidels he pursued them, and besieged the fort of Punganoor, occupying himself in opening trenches and approaches, and raising batteries, and in a very short time having battered down the walls by the fire from his guns took it, and then committing it to the charge of his own brave troops, he like a raging lion turned his face again to the field of battle, that is to the conquest of the Hill Fort before mentioned, but as this hill was surrounded by a frightful desart, and as the density of this forest was such, that no living creature could pass through the trees and bushes without the greatest difficulty and danger; — and, moreover, as the enemy had occupied the roads or paths on all sides, and had built towers from which they were ready to discharge their arrows and musketry, and make a vigorous defence; the Sipahdár during a month, and after the greatest labour and exertion, was unable to get even a glimpse of the cheek of the object of his desires (that is he made no progress), and on account of the insufficiency of his force,

being without resource, he addressed a letter to
the Presence and requested assistance. A Sipahdár of the name of Imám Khán with his
Kushoon was therefore appointed to his aid. On
the arrival there of the Khán above mentioned,
both the Sipahdárs consulted, and under the
guidance of some of the inhabitants of that part
of the country, they entered the forest or jungul
on two sides, and carried death and destruction
on the enemy, and they being defeated and dispersed, the hill was surrounded ; and after incre-
dible exertions for seventy days, the fort was taken.
The Poligar, however, with a number of his men
previous to this, avoiding the conflict, had fled and
sought refuge in the district of the Poligar of Chitore, and thereby escaped the vengeance of the
Sultán's troops. In about two or three months,
the two forts of the fugitive Poligar and all his
dependencies were taken, and committed to the
charge of the able servants of the presence, and
the two Sipahdárs having returned, and being
admitted to an audience of the Sultán, all the
plunder and the elephants and camels were passed
in review under his own inspection ; and the
Sipahdárs were honoured by the receipt of royal
presents and favours.

As the description of the mountain of Gywar

had been previously received from the Sipahdár
by the Sultán, he determined at this time to
inspect the hill himself, and therefore with his body
guard,ʳ certain of his friends, and the infantry of the
guard, he proceeded to Pungaloor, and a week
after to the hill, and having examined it, as he was
well pleased with its situation, the pioneers, able
stone-masons, and builders, were appointed to raise
the walls and buildings of a fort which was named
Ruhmaun Gurh.

Returning from this place, he honoured Nundi
Gurh with a visit, and named it Gurdoon Shukoh,ˢ
or the Terror of the World. The Sultán thence
proceeded to Dewun Hulli, and as that town was
the place of his birth, — *verse.* — " The earth of
one's own country is better than the throne of
Solomon" — that distinguished town, therefore,
was named Yousufabád, and a faithful servant was
left in charge of the fort, and strict orders were
given to him to repair the walls and buildings with
stone and mortar, and thence by pleasant easy
stages, in one month and fifteen days the Sultán
returned to his capital.

It is proper to mention here, that, as the Poligar
of Punganoor, by his evil fortune, according to the

ʳ Julow.

شكوه كردون ˢ

saying — *verse.* — " If thou contendest with thy
Lord and Master," — " wert thou the heavens thou
wouldest be turned upside down," — had been
severely punished by the Sultán's victorious troops,
and was now wandering in the desert of disgrace
and degradation, so in the same way the Poligar of
Muddun Pulli not well considering his future pros-
pects, followed the same path, and his territories
were also added to those of the Sultán.

CHAPTER V.

An account of the conquest of the Mountain Fort of Nurgoonda by the brave exertions of Kumruddín Khán, and his return
to the presence, with other events of the same year, A. D.
—1784.

As soon as Boorhanuddín, the Sipahsalar or commander-in-chief, had taken leave of the Sultán, he
marched by Chituldroog and Sanoor, and joined
Syud Ghuffar the Sipahdár in the vicinity of Dharwar, and having committed the charge of his right
and left wings to his bravest officers, he encamped
in the vicinity of the hill fort of Nurgoonda, and
apprized the mountain chief of his arrival, to take
possession of that fort, and also sent word to him
by messengers that if he was desirous to preserve
his country and property, he should immediately
quit the fort, and deliver it over to a Killadár
appointed by the Sultán, and then by manifestations
of regret for his misconduct enlighten the forehead of his obedience, and by employing Boorhanuddín's mediation, and every influence, and setting
forth his loyalty, his districts and property might

be restored to him — that otherwise he might be
certain he would give his life gratuitously to the
lower regions.[t] As he Kumruddín however received a scornful and bitter answer to this proposition, the fire of his pride and anger flamed
violently, and he marched on and encamped on a
river running south-west from the mountain, but at
the distance of seven or eight miles, and issued
orders to the faithful Sipahdárs, that is to Syud
Humíd and Syud Ghuffar to advance, and they
with great bravery moved on and enclosed the
mountain in a circle, and the infantry like mountain lions ascended and commenced the attack of
the fort on all sides, and by the fire of musketry
and artillery battered down the walls.

The mountain chief was however a brave man,
and his troops often sallied forth and attacked the
batteries, and killed many of those defending them.
As an example of their courage, one night finding
an opportunity, a small but brave detachment of
the garrison descended from the top of the mountain and attacked the pickets of the Sipahsalar's
army, stationed at the foot of the mountain, so
vigorously, that they killed the Bukshi, Sulábut
Khán, and two hundred horse. The gallant Sipahdárs, notwithstanding their increasing exertions to

ممالک نیران [t]

take this hill fort, still made no progress, and several assaults were made but without success. As
this happened to be the period of the hot season,
the want of water was felt to that degree, that
water-carriers brought water from the river on
which the army was encamped, on bullocks and
camels to the batteries at the foot of the mountain ;
and on account of the distance, also, in time of need
the men in the batteries could receive no succour
from the army. Notwithstanding this, the experienced Sipahdárs and the officers of the Ahshám,
or irregular infantry, exerted themselves in the
most zealous and honourable manner, and carried
on the batteries to the very foot of the walls. The
chief or Poligar of the fort, therefore, being alarmed
for the result, despatched an account of the critical
situation of his affairs to the chief of Mirch, and to
the Poona authorities, and requested their aid.

The Mirch chief accordingly sent five thousand
horse to his assistance. As this body of horse,
however, had encamped on a river, swelled by the
rains, and were waiting for a force of ten thousand
horse which had been despatched from Poona also
to the aid of the chief of Nurgoonda, the Sipahsalar
fearing the strength of so large a force of the enemy,
wrote a detailed account of their movements to the
Presence. The Sultán's ambassadors who were sta-

tioned at Poona also made him acquainted with these circumstances. The Sultán, therefore, despatched orders to Kumruddín Khán, directing him to proceed with his force to the aid of the Sipahsalar Boorhanuddín to oppose the Mahratta horse, and to take the fort.

It is proper, however, here to mention that Muhammad Pír Zadah, the son-in-law of Hulím Khán, the chief of Kirpa, finding an opportunity, and having by the pledge of valuable jewels obtained a large sum of money, assembled a body of four or five hundred horse and two thousand foot, and having made an agreement with the English of Mutchli Bundur (Masulipatam), and taking with him a battalion and two guns from Koottoor, he determined on attempting the re-conquest of the districts of Kirpa, and the reduction of the castles and forts of that country.— He therefore advanced and placed a garrison in the fort of Kuhmam, and slaying and plundering proceeded to Budweil. A party of infantry belonging to the Sultán were stationed in that fort, but they having been made favourable by bribery, with their permission or connivance he was allowed to send a party of his own men into the fort, and then he marched on to Kirpa. At this time Kumruddín Khán, by the orders of the Sultán arrived in that neighbourhood, and in conse-

quence in the vicinity of Phul Mamra, a severe battle
was fought between the two parties which continued
vigorously contested from the morning to midday,
and the brave men on both sides exerted themselves with the utmost gallantry. At length the
Khán, Kumruddín, determined to deceive and cir-
cumvent his enemies ; and of a sudden retired with
his troops from before them and concealed himself
in a wood, in front of which was a tank full of
water and a small hill in the midst of the tank, and
here he remained looking out for opportunities.
The Syud before mentioned, therefore, giving himself great credit for the victory he had achieved,
halted and encamped on the same spot of ground,
and the English officer commanding the battalion,
also discharging all apprehensions of his enemies
from his mind, and flattering himself they had no
power to oppose his attack and that they had fled,
encamped in the rear of the Syud's force. When,
therefore, two or three hours after this period, the
Syud's cavalry unarmed mounted their horses without saddles, and took them to the tank to water
them, and were each occupied with his own business ; of a sudden, the Kuzzaks of the brave Khán
(Kumruddín) taking advantage of this favourable
opportunity, charged them and gashed their breasts
with their swords and spears, and they, therefore,

fled towards their encampment and gave their
troops warning of the Khán's arrival, but the horse
of the Khán followed so close on their heels that
the whole of the force was trodden under the
hoofs of his cavalry, so that not a single man of
them remained alive, except the Syud and the
English officer, who with a thousand difficulties,
escaped with their lives from this place of slaughter.
The victorious Khán now took possession of the
forts of Budweil and Khummum, and having settled
the affairs of that quarter in the best manner possible, he remained with his troops and artillery ready
to chastise his enemies when the Sultan's order
arrived. The moment, therefore, this was received,
he marched with his troops and with four thousand
horse, forded the river Kishna, and in one night attack on the Mahratta horse, who were just ready to
cross over, drowned them in a sea of their own blood,
taking many of them prisoners. He then victorious marched towards the fort of Nurgoonda,
when he pitched his tents between the mountain
and the encampment of Boorhanuddín, and a Sipahdár named Shaíkh Imám, one of his own officers,
was sent to the assistance of the Sultán's faithful
servants. When the chief of the mountain heard
of the arrival of this force with its distinguished
commander, and the defeat of the Mahrattas, the

loins of his courage were broken, and as most of
the bravest infidels had been killed or wounded he
was unable to oppose further effectual resistance
to the army of Islám, and therefore weaning his
heart from the desire of possessing wealth and
dominion, and fearing for his life, after a week's
delay he despatched a message of peace and an
offer to surrender the fort to the Khán before mentioned.—He therefore apprized Boorhanuddín of
this message and having obtained his concurrence,
they in concert the next day despatched a Kowl
Nama, or the conditions of agreement, by the
hands of Syud Humíd and Mirza Hydur Alí Beg,
Risaldár, to the chief of the mountain and he was
brought down from the fort, and immediately with
his family and children placed in confinement, and
under the guard of the Kushoons of the Mirza and
Ahmed Beg sent to the presence. Some however
say that the daughter of the Poligar, who was one
of the most beautiful women of her time, after she
was honoured by reception into the Mussulman
faith and the performance of the marriage ceremony was received into the Hurum of the Sultán.
In short after the hill and fort were taken, the
Talooka was committed to the charge of an Amír,
a faithful servant of the Sirkar.

The Sipahsalar Boorhanuddín although he openly

appeared united and friendly with the Khán, still in secret entertained great enmity and hatred towards him, and used all kinds of arts in effecting the over-throw of his rank and dignity, and first because he had with his own troops defeated a large body of Mahrattas;—and next because the fort of Nur-goonda had surrendered after his arrival;—while he the Sipahsalar with all his exertions in six or seven months had done nothing. For these reasons he determined to accuse him of a violation or de-fection of his duty to his sovereign, and thereby make a display and merit of his own loyalty and zeal, and he therefore addressed a letter to the Sultán, stating that Kumruddín Khán, was a dis-affected person, and that it appeared that he through the medium of Mullik Esau Khán, alias Esau Mean Mehdivi, who was his secretary and counsellor, secretly maintained a correspondence with the Nizám of Hydurabád and Mushír ool Moolk Sohrab Jung—that besides this he was openly building a very large house in the Chudder Ghaut of Hydu-rabád, and that it was most likely he in a short time would abandon the service of the Sultán.

The Sultán without discriminating between friend and foe, as soon as the letter above mentioned arrived, recalled the Khán with his secretary and troops to the presence. This foolish man (the

Khán) however did not like to bring his secretary
to the Sultán, because during the period of his
Dewání or agency he had done many unworthy
acts, and had greatly oppressed and plundered the
poor, so much so indeed that the whole of the
peasantry weeping and wailing had fled to other
countries from his exactions and cruelty, for he
had taken all affairs of revenue or government
under his own direction, and decided on them
without asking the consent or pleasure of his
master. Of this the Sultán was aware. When
therefore the Khán proceeded to the presence, he
being afraid that some misfortune might befal him
in the event of an investigation into his conduct,—
conceiving that all had been done by him from
pure zeal for his (the Khán's) service,— he presented him a gift of a lakh of rupees, and without
the knowledge of any one sent him off by night to
Hydurabád, while he with his troops marched and
joined the Sultán. When however after his arrival
the Sultán called for the Dewán, the Khán answered
that he had taken leave to bring up his family and
dependants from Hydurabád.

This answer confirmed the bad opinion the Sultan
previously entertained and the brave Khán was
placed in confinement, and his troops incorporated
with the Sultán's army.

CHAPTER VI.

WHEN Zein ool Abidín Khán, Mehdivi, the Foujdár of Koorg, from his intimacy with the Sultán, and the confidence he reposed in him was placed in uncontrolled authority there, he filled all parts of the kingdom with rebellion, and regulated the affairs of the government according merely to his caprice and folly ; — insomuch that from the inherent vices of his disposition, he extended the hand of lust to the women of the peasantry, and compelled the handsomest among them to submit to his will and pleasure. In consequence of this tyrannical conduct, the whole of the people of Koorg advanced into the field of enmity and defiance, and every one in his own district prepared for battle, and Momuti Náír and Runga Náír, the ministers of the Poligar of that place, who eagerly looked out for such an opportunity to attack the Sultán's troops,

assembled all their retainers and peasantry, surrounded and besieged Zufurabád, plundered all
the country in its vicinity, and had reduced the
besieged to such extremities, that even during the
light of day they were afraid to quit the walls of
the fort. In addition to these misfortunes, they
had neglected to provide themselves with a sufficient stock of provisions and ammunition. The
Khán, who was the source and origin of these
troubles, at these occurrences began to be ashamed
of himself, he being shut up with the rest;
however, by disguising a Jasoos, or spy, he despatched him to the presence, with an account of
what had occurred and the insolence of the besiegers.

When the Jasoos had delivered the letter, and
and had detailed the situation of affairs, the Sultán
determined himself to punish the people of Koorg,
who had frequently before rebelled against his
government, and had blocked up the path of duty
and obedience with the thorns and stakes of sedition and rebellion, and had also given the troops
of the Sultán unceasing trouble.

He therefore issued orders to the quarter master
general, to proceed with the Tiger standard and
the blue Pavilion, and pitch them in the vicinity of Sultán Peeth, a town lately built at the

distance of one fursung and a half west from the
capital, and Zein ul Abidín Shoostri, Sipahdár
with his Kushoon and abundance of stores, and
two thousand Ahshám or irregular foot was sent
in advance as a warning to the rebels. The Sultán giving him orders to proceed without delay, by
forced marches to the fort of Zufurabád, and give
the rebels such a lesson as would in some measure
restore the peace of the country until the arrival
of the royal army, and likewise to inform the
inexperienced Foujdár there of the speedy arrival
of the Sultán, and to give him every assurance of
succour and support.

The Sipahdár above mentioned, who was a notorious coward, although, according to the Sultán's
orders he marched on quickly, and arrived at the
gate of the Ghaut ; still, as the rebels, as soon as
they became aware of his arrival attacked him on all
sides with their arrows and muskets, they soon dis-
sipated his senses and manhood. He, therefore,
being a person who had never before seen fighting,
but had spent his life in religious studies, lost all
confidence, and retired under the protection of the
Kotul or pass of Sudapoor ; and there fortified his
encampment, and notwithstanding all the Risaldárs
and Sipahdárs accompanying him, men who had
been trained to war under the instruction of the

brave commandant, Muhammad Alí, could say, in
prompting and urging him to move on, still the
Sipahdár, struck with fear, made the ague and
fever and a pain in the stomach his excuse, and refused to move forward a step. " Truly, — how can
the hard duties of soldiers be expected from luxu-
rious and effeminate men :" — when these circumstances became known to the Sultán, he bestowed
a few maledictions on his worthless officer, and
after making his arrangements and paying his troops
all which took up a fortnight, the dispenser of justice with twenty thousand regular infantry, twelve
thousand irregular foot, ten thousand good horse,
and twenty-two guns on the fifteenth of the month
of Zi-huj, with all the pomp and circumstance of
war marched towards that quarter.

   After the Sultán had arrived and encamped near
the stockade, or bound hedge of the Koorg
district, leaving all his horse at the Ghaut of Sudapoor, Puria Puttun, and Munzurabád; he with
his irregular foot, Kushoons and artillery, crossing
the Ghaut, threw himself like a raging lion into the
midst of that frightful forest, the Koorg country. —
Verses, — " What can I say of this wonderful wil-
derness." — " The pen trembles at its mention
alone." Its bamboo brakes intricate as the
woolly curls of an Abyssinian : — the roads or

paths as confused as the lines of the galaxy. *   The
high and low lands of that country unequal as
the souls of the generous and miserly. The
hills and valleys impassable. The low grounds
covered with rice crops as high as the waist.
The elephant of fancy is here immersed in its quag-
mires to the breast.   The boughs of many kinds of
trees such as the teak, the tall sandal, the white gum
and the ood, (a sweet smelling wood) reach with
their highest branches the Palm tree of Toba, (in Paradise), and the tendrils of the black pepper vine
spread the net of deceit over all other shrubs and trees.
The fields of Kakila, that is to say, cardamums, like
fields of wheat and barley blooming over hill and
dale, — cinnamon trees, also, like the light and clouds
of the heavens distilling life and vigour over all the
herbs of the field — and the fruits of the gardens,
such as falsa, (a berry used in making sherbet)
citrons, the custard apple, the Burheil, and jamoo,
(a kind of plum) the plantain, are the dispensers of
honey and sugar, to the bitter palates of the unfortunate.   The rivers in that country like the eyes
of the sorrowful, always overflowing.   The tanks
and reservoirs on the roads like the eyes of the for-
saken, full day and night.   The bride of the ver-

* Some copies of the work have — " as the curly ringlets of
a bride."

dant earth drowned in the dew of modesty, veils
herself from the eyes of the sun in the dark shades
of the forest;—parterres of the buds, or flowerets,
of the Mehdí, Velvet, and hundred-leaved, roses,
always blossoming, like wanton girls, take off their
modest veils to shew their beauties. Wild elephants
resembling mountains, both male and female, like
troops of buffaloes wander about at their perfect
freedom, and the young elephants like young Abys-
sinians making chowkans (a kind of cricket bat)
of their trunks play at ball.[x]

Most of the towns and villages of that country are
placed under hills, or are concealed among the trees;
— they are surrounded by strong walls, in which
many apartments and houses are built, and also in
the enclosed space, and they are secured by a deep
ditch dug all round,—this is to protect their houses,
for in the dark nights the elephants frequently make
an attack on their villages and plunder and destroy
them; — this, therefore, preserves the inhabitants
and their property in safety. The men are mostly
of a brown complexion, or the colour of wheat,
but some are black — they are tall in stature; their
clothing consist in a very dirty shirt, double, reaching from the neck to the ancles, and until this shirt

[x] I should have left out most of this poetical description of
Koorg, but that I did not consider myself justified in curtailing
the work.

is worn to rags, they never think of changing it : —
they use a handkerchief, black or white, tied round
their loins, and wear a leathern cap on their heads.
The soldiers, however, never stir out of their houses
or towns without a matchlock with the match
lighted in their hands, and a broad knife which they
call kurkutti, fastened round their waists.   The
women are beautiful, and in bloom and delicacy, the
envy of the beauties of China and Choghul, and in
elegance of form and gait, silvery complexions, and
loveliness of feature, they rival the maids of Turkis-
tán and Persia. In that wild country, which is however, beautiful as the garden of Paradise, they move
about gracefully as the divine Hooris, — they, however, are very ill and indelicately clothed, — one
cloth about ten or twelve feet long, is wound round
them, reaching from the navel to the knee, and
a white handkerchief about three feet square is
thrown on their tender breasts, the treasury of love.
This dress destroys the effect of their beauty.   The
men of this country are cold, and passionless, in
regard to women ; but the women on the contrary
are eager and ardent in their intercourse with men.
Historians of old relate that formerly in the neighbourhood of Akrubnar, (Nar, or rather Nad[r] in the
language of that country, signifying a town), it was

[r] Nad as Ramnad. &c.

a foolish custom, but one considered in their pagan
religion both proper and meritorious, that if there
happened to be four brothers in one house, one only
of them married, and the others cohabited with the
woman so married by turns, one every night, and
some even say, that all four remained with her
every night,ª — the offspring of these marriages
were divided among the brethren.

When, however, the deceased Nawáb (Hydur)
conquered this country, he abolished this abomi-
nable custom, and seizing many of the women, he
gave them to his own soldiers.

But to return, — a description of the cold here
makes the pen before it begins to write, stiff, as if
it were plunged into the frozen sea, — and the
tongue of truth at describing the temperature is
with fear and astonishment congealed like ice, notwithstanding it is covered with the posteen of the
lips,ª what can it say therefore. The sun with all
its heat fearing the influence of the cold, every day
covers his head with a counterpane of clouds and
hurries away from this country : ᵇ — the fast travel-
ling moon also every night from a similar fear
hides her face in the blue veil of the heavens. This,

ª Julius Cæsar says the same of the Ancient Britons.
ª Moustaches.
ᵇ In the original this is written merely to shew the ability and
learning of the author.

however which has been written, is the description
of the summer. God protect us from the winter
and rainy seasons, — for during six months in the
year, the clouds of Azur (the ninth month,) pour
their showers over the whole of that country, and
the earth like the eyes of the oppressed, is filled
with water, and from the evening, until two hours of
the day have arisen, (seven or eight o'clock in the
morning), the vapours of the falling dew, like the
sighs of the afflicted, cover hill and dale, and many
straight well made active young men from the
violence of the cold having lost the warmth or use
of their limbs, sleep in their narrow huts like a
bow with their feet and breasts doubled up together. For six months the labourers or cultivators
of the soil of that country, covered from head
to foot with an old cloth or blanket, work for nine
or ten hours a day, but all this time they are
subject to the bites of leeches which are produced
from the roots of the trees by excessive rain, and
remain among the leaves and branches, and these
in number, like locusts thirsting for blood, rise
and fix themselves on the bodies of men and
cattle to their great injury, and never quit them
until they are filled with their blood; — besides
these, there are an infinite number of serpents of
all kinds, and the most poisonous scorpions, and if

these bite any living creature, its life quits the body so instantly, that even the Angel of Death is not prepared to receive it.

But to proceed : — when the pious Sultán entered that Jungulistán or country of forests, by the route of the Turkul Ghaut, he encamped on this side the gate of the stockade, called Mundul. The next day he gave orders to his two Sipahdárs with their Kushoons to assault the stockade gate, before which the infidels had dug a deep ditch and had built a wall on each flank, and from these with their arrows and matchlocks they completely blocked up the road : — they accordingly commenced the action, but on this day the infidels displayed the utmost intrepidity and not only repelled their assaults, but drove the two Kushoons before them and killed and wounded the greatest part.

The conquering Sultán however with his victorious troops by a route by which the wind and rain could scarcely penetrate, now with the rapidity of lightening fell upon the infidels, and despatched a great number of them to the infernal regions. On the other side, the French under Monsieur Lally and the Assud Ilahi Risalas or regiments of Chelahs,* made numbers of these Pa-

* Slaves brought up by the late Nawáb and trained for service by the Sultán, and when formed into regiments called by him Assud Ilahi.

gans food for the musket and bayonet;—on the other flank also, the infantry of the body guard[d] with the greatest intrepidity took up their enemies one by one on the points of their spears or bayonets and threw them head foremost into the depths of hell, and many of the infidels were made prisoners. Notwithstanding all this, they still stood firm and made many vigorous attacks on the Sultán's army and dispersed them. At this time, therefore, the select of the body guard and certain of the Sipahdárs seeing the bravery of the enemy, assembled those who still remained, and determining by successive charges to make an impression, threw themselves at once on the enemy. In the twinkling of an eye, therefore, the bonds which kept together the infidels were broken and they lost their stability and firmness, and placed their feet in the desert of flight.

The soldiers of the Sultán's army now, therefore, closely pursued them and troops of them were slain with the unpitying sword. When the Sultán had thus conquered his enemies, he advanced and encamped in the vicinity of Hulkulinar, and the Shoostri who has been before mentioned, when he saw the plain cleared of the enemy, to do away with the impression of his former misconduct made

[d] Julowdárs.

an attack on the village of Khooshalpoor and plundered and burned it, making prisoners of a great
number of the infidels, with their wives and children;—he then returned to the presence. From
this place now, agreeably to the Sultán's orders,
four Risalas, or regiments, with a large supply of
stores and provisions, marched to the fort of Zuffurabád (Mudgiri), while the Sultán himself remained encamped where he was until the thir-
teenth of the month of Mohurrum il Huram. On
the fifteenth of that month, A.H. 1199, the Sultán marched by several stages to the capital of
Koorg, and encamped on the eastern side of the
town, by the road, by which, according to the
orders of the Sultán, the Amírs and Kháns had
entered the jungles, and with hatchets and saws
had daily cut away and-burned the jungle to the
distance of three miles, and in this way had cleared
the country to the distance of seven or eight miles.
In these operations the tenants of the jungles had
been reduced to great extremities and in different
battles also of the infidels two or three thousand
men had been destroyed.

When, therefore, the chiefs of Koorg saw the
signs of weakness and debility on the forehead of
the condition of their men, and that they no longer
had the power to oppose the army of Islám, they

dispersed to all parts of the mountains and jungles, and sought refuge in the most difficult and inaccessible parts of the country.

The conquering Sultán now therefore appointed and despatched his Amírs and Kháns with large bodies of troops to punish these idolaters and reduce the whole of the country to subjection. As for instance, Monsieur Lally was sent for that purpose to the Ilaichee or Cardamum Ghauts, (the western Ghauts according to Colonel Marriott) and the Kushoon of the Shoostri with another was sent under the command of Hussein Alí Khan Bukhshi towards Akrubnar. The rest of the Sipahsirdárs that is to say Mír Mahmood, Imám Khán, &c. were despatched to the Thul Kauveri, and Khooshalpoora, and for two or three months, the Sultán remained encamped on the same ground. The Bukhshi before mentioned however by good management and exertion carried distress and confusion among the rebels of that quarter (Akrubnad), and in a short time attacked and destroyed many of their towns, returning with eight thousand men and women with their children prisoners. In the same way Monsieur Lally collected from the Ilaichee Mountains an immense crowd of these wild men, like a flock of sheep or a herd of bullocks, and returned with them to the presence. The Sultán after this moved forward and pitched his tents and standards on ground to the southward of the hill of Thul Kauveri, (the fountain or source of the River Kauveri, arising from the same hill) and despatched his troops in advance, giving them orders to pursue the rebels, that is to capture their chiefs.

The brave Sipahdárs in consequence advanced to the attack on all sides, and as they knew that to cut off these infidels, the seed of disobedience and rebellion, was the policy of the Sultán's government, and likewise that most profitable to themselves, they with great labour and exertions captured and brought in troops upon troops of the rebels, and in the course of seven months and a few days eighty thousand, men, women and children were made prisoners. At length both the before men-tioned chiefs were taken on the Ilaichee Moun-tains by the exertions of Monsieur Lally. The war, therefore, was now at an end and the rest of the disobedient being humbled, became enrolled among the faithful servants of the Sultán. The Sultán after making arrangements for the security of his conquests, and the erection of several wooden or stockaded forts (called in this country Lukkur Kote) being now free from all apprehension, re-

turned victorious to his capital by the route of
Sudapoor.

Of the two chiefs, one Mumoti Naír in a short
time died,* and Runga Naír was honoured by being
circumcised and made a Mussulman by the Sultán,
and named Shaíkh Ahmud, and appointed a Risaldár. — The Sultán also adopted him as his son.
Ballia Banoo the Queen of Kunianore (Cananore)
who was of the Mapilu tribe, paid her respects to
the Sultán while he was encamped at Thul Kauveri,
and brought with her the tribute due for two years,
with elephants, horses and other valuables as pre
sents; — and she in return was dismissed with
dresses of honour and other royal presents.

When the Sultán arrived at Seringaputtun,
the prisoners taken in the country of Koorg,
who had been all made Mussulmans and were
styled Ahmudees, were formed into eight Risalas
or regiments, and veteran officers were appointed
to train and discipline them, and they with very
little labour having instructed these wild men,
soon made them perfect in their military exercises and movements. About this time the Sultán
caused gorgets of gold, silver and jewels to be
made, and they were presented to the officers of

* Not a natural death I fear.

horse and foot, the Assud Ilahi and Ahmudi regiments, according to their different ranks, and the uniforms of these regiments being also made up of tiger cloth, (a new invention in weaving) they were clothed in it. The names of the twelve months and the cycle of sixty years were changed in contradistinction to the Arabian names, all which however shall be detailed, please God, on some future occasion. The names also of a number of forts were changed in the same manner; — as for instance; — Chitul Droog, was called Furrokh Yab Hissar; Gootti, Fyze Hissar; Bullari, Sumr Puttun; Punoogoondi, Fukhrabád; Pao Gurh, Khutmi Gurh; — The Souba Sura, Roostumabád; — but this being the old name was, therefore, merely renewed, or restored; — Nundi Gurh, Gardoon Shukoh; Dewun Hulli, Yousufabád; Pungalore, Darussurroor; Makri, Sawan Gurh. The fort of Bul, Munzurabád; Koorg, Zufurabád; Kalikote, Islamabád; Dindigul, Khalikabád; Sunkli Droog, Muzuffarabád; Kishingiri, Fulk il azum; Mysore, Nuzzurbár; — and in this manner in all matters new terms, or new inventions were introduced. About this time also, from the whole of the Sultán's servants, six or seven thousand men of the Shaíkh and Syud tribes were selected and despatched to Koorg to re-people that district: —

The air and water, however, not agreeing with them, some fell sick with the fever and ague, and after repeated applications to the presence were allowed to return; — but some with whom the climate agreed, remained there.

CHAPTER VII.

The invasion of Mysore by the Mahrattas and the chief of Hydurabád with the intention to subdue the territories of the Khodádád Kingdom, and the conquest by them of certain forts of that State in their neighbourhood, and the march of the victorious Sultán to repel his enemies by the route of Adhooni, and the conquest of that place in the year 1199 Hijri, with other matters, A.D. 1785.

WHEN the Ambassadors of the Sultán, who previous to this time had proceeded to Poona with presents and ten lakhs of rupees, in money, arrived there, and had visited the chief (the Paishwa) and the minister, Nana Furnavees and had made an offer of the foregoing presents and money, they refused to receive them and peremptorily rejected the whole.

The reply of the Sultán which has been before mentioned, " that he had inherited a few guns and muskets from his father and had always kept them in readiness," remained fixed in the Paishwa's heart like a thorn, and he, therefore, in these plans (the rejection of the presents, &c.) united in heart and hand with Nizám Alí Khán and despatched

orders to all parts to collect his Amírs, or chief
officers. Accordingly in a very short time all the
Amírs of Poonah with their contingents of troops
and warlike stores assembled, and Nizám alí Khán
conformably to his **agreement**, with his chiefs such
as Mushír ul Moolk, Syfe Jung, Teigh Jung, &c.
and the whole of his army consisting of forty thousand horse and fifty thousand foot, marched from
Hydurabád and by the route of Bidur proceeded
towards Budami, the fort of which is the frontier
station of the Sultán's dominions in that direction.

The Mahrattas also with eighty thousand horse,
forty thousand foot and fifty guns of heavy calibre
and vast quantities of warlike stores, being all in
readiness, marched and arrived at Budami. The Ambassadors of the Sultán therefore received their dismission, from that place, and the two Potentates (the
Paishwa and Nizám) now met and having consulted
together, determined to attack the forts of Mysore;
and first gave orders to besiege the fort of Budami
which was however held by a brave officer. The
Amírs therefore of these Princes exerted themselves
strenuously in the attack of the fort, and in raising
batteries and battering down the walls, and also by
continually repeated assaults,—but notwithstanding
they lost thousands upon thousands of brave men
in these operations, it was taken at last by capitu-

lation only, after a siege of nine months. The confederates, however, after repairing the fort still remained there, in order to collect supplies and stores, despatching their Amírs to all quarters to reduce and take possession of other forts and towns, and accordingly the said Amírs with a large force marched and obtained possession of Dharwar and Jalihul, by a bribe of thirty thousand rupees. It is proper to mention here that the governor of these two forts was a certain Hydur Buksh, a Rafizi or Sheea, a man who had but a short time before been Khán Samán or house-steward to the Amír ul Omra, the son of Muhammad Alí Khán, Suráj ud Dowla; — and at first was a confidential servant, but at length having misapplied and stolen a large sum of the money of his master, and being consequently afraid of punishment, he deserted from him and sought refuge in the protection of the Sultán, and was appointed to the command of these forts, ; — this man following the path of ingratitude gave them up for the amount specified, to the Sultán's enemies ; — while, he himself with his followers and property took the road to Poona. In the same way Gujindur Gurh, Nolegoonda, Nurgoonda, &c. indeed the whole of that side of the River Tungbhudra was surrendered to the enemy. The commanders of these forts being treacherous scoun-

drels, who seduced from their duty by the promise
of increased rank and pay, and the payment of
ready money in bribes, joined the enemy. The
Poligars of that quarter as the chief of Sir Hutti,
Dumul, Kunukgiri and Anigoonda, also joined and
assisted the enemy. When the Sultán's spies reported these circumstances to him, and his faithful
Amírs, and chief officers, advised and entreated him
to march to oppose his enemies, he immediately ordered the assembly of his army and the different
departments, and on the sixth of the month of
Shaban ul Muazum of this year, with a fine well disciplined army consisting of six Kushoons or brigades
of regular infantry (a Kushoon is about two thousand men) three Mowkubs of horse, (the Mowkub is
a regiment of regular cavalry of about four hundred
horses and men according to Kirkpatrick)[f] ten thousand irregular foot, thirty thousand good horse and a
park of twenty-two heavy guns, marched to Bun-
galore and ordered the attendance of the Poligars.
The Moonshis or secretaries therefore quickly wrote
out orders directing them to join immediately with
their troops, provisions and stores, and promising to
remit their tribute until the conclusion of the war

[f] For a more detailed explanation of these terms, I beg to
refer to the select letters of Tipú Sultán, translated by Col.
Kirkpatrick, p. 958 of the Appendix.

(with the Mahrattas and the Nizám). The Poligars of the different countries, such as the chiefs of Rai Droog, Hurpun Hulli, and others despatched their contingents of troops to the presence according to custom, but the chiefs themselves pretending to be sick remained at home.

But to return,—after the conclusion of the festival of the Lílut ul Barát ᵉ, and the payment of the whole army, the Sultán marched by great Balapoor, Hindoopoor and Pao Gurh to the river Makri, where he halted two days, and leaving his heavy baggage and followers to the care of Purnia, the Mutsuddí, or clerk of the Toshu ʰ Khána, the Sultán with his horse lightly equipped, by a forced march moved on to the vicinity of Hunoor where he encamped. — The next day he marched on to the town of Kubkul, two Kose east from Bullari, where he encamped part of one night, but moving on during the night ; at day break the next morning his advanced guard suddenly appeared in front of the hill of Adhooni, and the Sultán and his cavalry halted and rested themselves at the village of Gulbayen. The governor of Adhooni, Mohábut Jung, (the son of Shuja ul Moolk Busálut Jung,) who

ᵉ ليلة البرات

ʰ توش is synonymous with زاد and signifies the wallet or provisions of a traveller.

was married to the daughter of Nizám Alí Khán, (the Subadár of the Deckan) had his family with him having been lately appointed to the government of that part of the country.

As soon, therefore, as he heard of the arrival of the victorious army, being greatly alarmed, he deputed his minister Assud Alí Khán to the presence, and in the meantime taking advantage of the opportunity, despatched the whole of his wealth with his women to the mountains. When the envoy presented himself to the Sultán he in the name of his master entreated the Sultán would desist from his purpose to injure or molest him. The Sultán replied, that in his heart he had entertained no enmity to his master, but, that as the Nawáb (the Nizám) without cause had manifested hostility towards him, and had joined the Brahmans (the Paishwa, &c.) and was seeking the overthrow and destruction of his state, he would soon see the difference between his (the Sultán's) friendship and fidelity and their treachery and violation of treaties: —that, independent of this, they (the Nizám) had abandoned the ties of faith and religion, and had joined the ancient enemy of his house, and with a large army had invaded and taken possession of the territories of a Mussulman Sovereign, and had carried their enmity to that degree that Idolators had

plundered and burned the Musjids or mosques and
houses of Mussulmans and the poor people of the
country, and had raised the flag of rapine and
desolation in the territory of the Khodadád ; —
that it would be good policy, therefore, that they
(the Sultán and Mohábut Jung) should strengthen
the foundations of friendship and unite in repelling
and doing away with those who were shaking the
chain of hatred and enmity — (in the original an
allusion to the chain of gold in front of Noushirwan's
palace, shaken by those who demanded justice) or
that they should meet and consult in this matter, and
if he Mohábut Khán chose, he might remain where
he was, sending a body of his best troops under the
command of his own officers to join and aid the Sultán's forces. For that he (the Sultán) had bound
up his loins in this religious war in order to establish
Islamism on a firm basis, to obtain the favor of God,
and ensure the peace and safety of God's people.
As the governor (Mohábut Khán) did not however agree to the Sultán's propositions and failed in
coming to present his respects to him, and also
prepared to resist and defend himself, the Sultán
to give him an example of what he could do and
to frighten him, the morning after that day, gave
orders to the Sipahdárs to attack the town, and
they assaulted and took it, and swept it with the

besom of destruction, — they did not however suc-
ceed in bringing the governor to the right path,
and, therefore, on both sides the fire of war was
kindled, and the soldiers of the victorious army
and the chief of the ordnance department, turned
their faces to the reduction of the fort, high as the
heavens, and having encompassed it on all sides,
raised batteries, dug their approaches and pushed
on their attacks chiefly from the garden containing
the tomb of Busálut Jung, and from the tank at
the Tomul gate, — from thence they kept up a
continual fire of cannon and mortars ; — still, however, the Sultán's compassionate heart never intended the conquest of this fort, but what he did
was merely to awaken the solicitude of the chief
of Hydurabád (the Nizám) for the honour of his
relation and the safety of his daughter, shut up in
the fort, and the siege of the fort was undertaken
in the hope that by this means he might be in-
duced to offer terms of accommodation, and desist
from the ruin of the poor people of the country.
Otherwise if the Sultán had seriously intended to
take the fort he could have taken it with ease the
first day, and also the governor with his women
and wealth, as will be seen from the following
statement ; — for when, in the morning, the Sultán's
army attacked, and entered the city and pene-

trated, firing vollies to the gate of the fort, it was open for any one to enter, and when the inhabitants of the city, who fled to the fort from fear of losing their lives like so many crows or kites, were shouting, screaming and crowding to get to the gate, of the garrison not a single man was to be seen either on the bastions, or walls; — the fear of the lion-like Ghazies having seized on them. At seeing this, some of the Sultán's friends and Amírs represented to him that this was the very time to take the fort; that he should not allow his enemies leisure to rub their eyes and awaken from their sleep of neglect, and, that if he would give orders they would take the fort, and bring Mohábut Khán willing or unwilling to the presence.

Roostum Jung, that is to say Monsieur Lally the French officer, also repeatedly submitted this to the Sultán. The Sultán, however, pretended indifference to the matter and said do not attempt it, on any account; please God to-day or to-morrow, or perhaps in a week, or at furthest a month, he Mohábut Khán will come out and surrender himself with his hands tied. The writer of these lines was present at this siege; — but to return, — after mid-day the besieged governor gave orders for the regulation and security of the fort, and, assembling his soldiers, amounting to near seven

thousand men, horse and foot, took the duties or
direction of the defence upon himself. Lal Khán
and Saudullah Khán, Surkheíl of the Kaim Khanees,
who had command of four hundred Jaunbazes, were
stationed at the gates and kept themselves ready
to repel the assaults of the victorious army, and
each side laboured hard in all warlike arts to deceive the other. When the Nizám of Hydurabád
heard of these occurrences he refused to eat or
sleep, and the forced march of that lion of the
forest of valour (Tipú Sultán) and the attack of
Adhooni deprived him of his senses. Having
therefore apprized the Paishwa of these circumstances, they held a consultation on the subject;—
some of the more experienced and wise among
them, said that seeing that the frontier fort Budami
which was not very strong was taken by capitulation only, after the labours of two armies for nine
months, during which the smoke of the guns and
muskets had been sufficient to dry up the brains of
those employed in the siege, and that in one year
they had actually done nothing more;— what
could be expected from their future operations?
that since the troops of the Sultán in the absence
of their master were not slack in fighting, what
would they not do in his presence? that the best
thing they could do, therefore, was to appoint a

number of officers with troops to lay waste the
country and that the two princes should return
to their capitals. This advice of the Amírs being
approved by the princes, and their policy highly
applauded, the Nizám of Hydurabád on his part
appointed Mushír ul Moolk, Syfe Jung and others
with a large body of troops to the relief of Adhooni
and the chief of Poona, (the Paishwa) appointed
Yuswunt Rao Holkar, Purusram the chief of
Mirch, Hurri Punt Phurkia, Rastia Mahratta and
other Amírs, with all the horse, foot and artillery
to the aid of the Amírs of Hydurabád and the devastation of the Sultán's territories, and the two
princes under pretence of ill health returned to
their own capitals, that is to say Hydurabád and
Poona.

The Sultán at hearing this intelligence was much
encouraged and determined now to take the fort
of Adhooni, and to punish the governor who had
so contumaciously refused to listen to his suggestions or advice, and in consequence issued orders
to his officers to breach the walls, and they occupied themselves in battering the defences and
assaulting the fort, one month and twenty days.

The site of the fort, however, and the strength
of the walls (which were built by Musaood Khán an
Amír of the Adil Sháhi dynasty, as has been de-

tailed in the author's work, Tuzkirut il Beladwa il
Ahkam, in the second Ourung) were of that description, that the dust was not shaken upon one of its
dunghills by the fire of the guns, nor were the
walls to be breached by cannon or mortars, the
fire therefore was of no avail. After some parts of
the walls, however, were in a slight degree injured by the fire of the guns, the lions of the forest
of valour, according to the Sultán's orders, made a
vigorous assault on several sides ; that is to say, Syud
Sáhib and Kotabuddín Dowlut Zai, from the bury-
ing ground of Busálut Jung ; Monsieur Lally and
Imám Khán Sipahdár from the Tamool gate, and
Hussein Khán, Boozai ; and Muhammad Hulím
from the hill of Huzar Zeena. These having
planted ladders against the wall attempted to esca-
lade the fort. The garrison who were famous for
the obstinacy of their resistance, and for their hardy
endurance of the labours and hardships of the siege,
crowded round the works to oppose them and manfully repelled their assailants, and a great number
of them fell by the sword : the cause being that the
ladders which had been made according to the
instructions of the Hurkurus, or spies, were found
too short compared with the height of the walls,
and the brave soldiers, although they abandoned
the ladders and strove to mount the walls by

driving in iron pegs or spikes, still failed, and that
day were entirely unsuccessful, for the garrison
with the sword, arrow and musket, effectually
stopped their progress, and near two thousand
brave soldiers lost their lives on that occasion. At
the result of this assault the Sultán was much
grieved, and several of the Hurkuras and spies
were put to death.

For some days after this, therefore, the troops
did nothing but light up the fire of war, and from
morn till night the flames of contention blazed
high, and again ladders were prepared long and
strong, and they with iron pins and ropes were all
in readiness, when Mushír ul Moolk and Syfe Jung,
&c. accompanied by the Mahratta army, arrived
to the succour of their fort. The Sultán on becoming aware of their arrival, not liking war on
both flanks (or rather in his front and rear) abandoned his batteries, and changed his ground, encamping with his rear to the Black mountains,
and there having stationed guards and pickets on
all sides, remained in readiness for action. Two
days after a severe action was fought between the
outposts, or advanced parties, of the Sultán and
the Mahrattas ; — the cause being the folly and
incapacity of Hydur Hussein, Bukshi Silahdár, who
with a body of seven hundred horse belonging to
Gházi Khán, Bede (an officer who never au-

H

thorized any such movement), from conceit attacked a force of ten thousand Mahratta horse,
but at length finding he could not resist this mighty
force, he was obliged to retreat.

The brave Ghází Khán, however, with the same
body (seven hundred horse), still kept his ground
against the ten thousand, and for two hours displayed the utmost gallantry, but from apprehension
of disgrace, he despatched the rash Bukhshi to the
presence, in charge of his son Kudr Khán, and in
the mean time, after distinguishing himself in the
most heroic manner without aid or succour, and
being wounded, he was obliged reluctantly to quit
the field : — The Mahrattas, however, followed him
and killed some of his party, and two or three
hundred of his men with their horses were taken
prisoners by them, and they then returned. Kudr
Khán, however, with two hundred Janbazes, after
escorting the Bukhshi to the camp, charged the
enemy and recovered eighty horse of his own
troop, and made prisoners of fifty of the enemy's
horse, and brought them to the presence. In the
course of this action, Lumchur the Kuzzak, and
Manna Chowdhuri, made a sudden Chuppao attack,
and captured two elephants, eight camels, and fifty
ponies, from the Moghuls of Hydurabád. The
Sultán on hearing this, immediately beat to arms,
and with all his troops marched rapidly, on their

heels the fire of his artillery opening so suddenly
that the outposts of the enemy fell back on their
main bodies, and both their armies fell into great
confusion, and sought refuge under cover of the
city, and fort, and from that time never returned
to the field of battle. The Sultán, therefore, remained until evening, with his troops formed in
order of battle, expecting their advance; but, at
length, leaving two Kushoons as pickets in front
of the enemy, he returned to his ground of encampment.

The morning of the next day, Mushír ul Moolk
and the others having consulted, after a great deal
of contention, took the governor of Adhooni (he
being persuaded to consent) with his property and
family to the fort of Raichore — when the spies
reported this to the presence, the Sultán immediately detached Mír Sadik with a body of troops to
take possession of the fort and stores, while he himself followed the steps of the confederates to the
river Tungbhudra, eight fursungs distant, and
took some of their stragglers prisoners and some
baggage which had been left behind; and then
returned and encamped on the north side of the
fort. The Mír before mentioned, having taken possession of the fort and the palace of Mohábut Khán,
placed all the valuable property left by that chief
with some boxes locked up with great care, on his

camels and elephants, and sent them to the presence.   When, however, the Mutsuddies (civil
servants) of the Tosha Khána opened these boxes,
they found nothing in them but old slippers and
shoes (intended as a manifestation of contempt for
the Sultán) they, therefore, surmised that perhaps
the governor of the fort, among his other avoca-
tions exercised the profession of a churum doze or
cobler, or that he had collected some tax (in kind)
from the houses of the shoemakers; or, perhaps
that he had collected them in the way of trade,
to send them for sale to Hydurabád.

On the representation of these circumstances to
the Sultán, he was much displeased at the stupidity
and folly of the Mír, and ordered him to examine
with his own eyes, all the property and articles of
value, and select only such as were worthy, and
send them to the Sultán, and to leave those belonging to the shoemakers or leather dressers where
they were.   The whole, therefore, of the wardrobe,
the armoury and the tents, &c. of Busálut Jung, were
taken and deposited in the stores of the Sultán.
After the accomplishment of these measures, the
lower fort was laid in ruins, and Kotub uddín Khán
Dowlut Zai, was appointed to the charge of that
Souba.

CHAPTER VIII.

The march of the victorious army to the discomfiture of the
Mahrattas then plundering and laying waste the country on the
other side the river Tungbhudra, and an account of the capture
of Kunchun Gurh and Kupli or Kopli; the passage of the river
by the victorious army, and the battles there fought with the
Mahrattas in the same year, Hijri, 1199.

As soon as the Sultán was set free by the conquest of Adhooni, he having in view the chastisement of the Mahrattas, marched by the route of
Kunchun Gurh, and despatched a party of horse
in advance, to take prisoner the widow of the Poligar of that place; — the Poligar himself having
died a short time previously. His wife, therefore,
whose name was Tunguma, governed in his place;
but at that time had taken her feet out of the circle
of obedience, and loyalty to the Sultán, and sometime before this in the hope of an increase of
territory, and wealth, had entered into negotiations for herself, with the chief of the Mahrattas,
through the medium of Hurri Punt Phirkia: —
when, however, this woman heard of the Sultán's
intention, she immediately fled by night, with a

few slave girls and servants, and crossing the river
Tungbhudra, escaped. Her son, however, whose
name was Moodkum Koor, and about ten or twelve
years of age, was taken prisoner in the small fort
of Surkah, his residence; and was honored by
being circumcised and made a Moslim, and he
thence forward received the name of Alí Murdán
Khán, as will be seen in the account of his family
given by the author of these lines, in his work
called the Tuzkirut il Belád wa il Ahkám [1] in the
eleventh Ourung : — It will be seen there, that
the above named (Alí Murdán) after some time
was married to the daughter of Khán Jehán
Khán, who also was an adopted son of the late
Nawáb, and originally the son of a Brahman,
the Desepandia of Kolar, who in his youth being
ill treated by his school master, of his own pleasure, the great and true guide shewing him the
way, reached the presence of the deceased Nawáb, and became a Mussulman and his wife also,
after arriving at the years of discretion, of her own
free will, and after obtaining permission of her
father and mother, embraced the religion of her
husband, and thereby secured to herself happiness
in both worlds.

تذكرة البلاد والاحكام [1]

The Sultán from this place marched on and arrived in the neighbourhood of Soondoor : — the
governor of that fort was named Govind Rao, the
nephew of the celebrated Morar Rao, who after
the capture of his uncle, had retired to Poona,
and there representing to the Paishwa the ruin that
had befallen him, solicited a recommendatory letter
in the name of the Nawáb, and having obtained it,
returned to the presence. The Nawáb being na-
turally compassionate and indulgent, and desirous
also to oblige the Paishwa, after taking security that
he, Govind Rao, should in no circumstances violate
his engagements with the government, continued
him in the possession of the fort of Soondoor. At
this time, however, he had quitted the path of recti-
tude and had united with the Mahrattas, but when
he heard of the march of the Sultán's troops, the
flight of the lady before mentioned (Tunguma) and
the condition of her son, he lost the use of his
senses, and fled to the Mahratta army with his
servants and dependants. Talooka Soondoor with
its dependencies was, therefore, taken possession
of, without opposition by the servants of the Sultán.
After the necessary arrangements for the security
of this place, the Sultán exalted as the heavens,
with his army, in number, equalling the number of
the stars, marched towards Kopli. The governor

of that place who was a relation of the rebel Poligar of Kunukgiri, strengthened his fort, and remained ready for the attack, and notwithstanding
the Sultán's Amírs strove to advise and direct
him ; it was all of no use[k] — according, therefore,
to the orders of the Sultán, the brave Sipahdárs
and the French officer M. Lally assaulted the fort
on both flanks and took it by storm, — and for an
example to the rest of the infidels it was sacked,
and the women, both Mussulman and Hindu, violated by the soldiers, and money and valuables to
a great amount taken from the houses of the merchants, bankers, and weavers or cloth makers, of
the people of Islám, who are called Momin, and
many also of the women of that tribe, from fear of
violation by the soldiery, threw themselves into
the river Tungbhudra, which at that time was
raging with the violence of the rains, and pe-
rished : — the governor of the fort was also killed.

When, however, the Sultán heard of the violation of the women he punished his soldiers severely,
and issued orders, strictly prohibiting such exces-
ses in future. — From this place the Sultán now
marched on to the neighbourhood of the town of
Huspeenth depending on the Poligar of Hurpunhully, and halted their four days.   In these marches

[k] He knew the value of their advice.

and halts the month of Ramzan (the lent of the Mussulmans) was completed, and after the fulfilment of the devotional duties of the Eed il Fitr, or the conclusion of the fast and the customary banquets and rejoicings, the Sultán marched and pitched the tents of his army on the bank of the Tungbhudra even with the Ford or Ghaut of Goruknath ; — as it happened, however, to be the period of the swelling of the river, some delay took place in crossing it : — in that time, therefore, the Mahrattas subdued and took possession of all the country, on the other side the river ; and with the intention to attack the Sultán, raised their inauspicious standards opposite to him, and fortified with guns and musketry the ford of the river against the passage of his army ; and they also despatched an officer with a large body of troops to capture the Hill Forts of Gopul and Bahadúr Bundah. This officer, therefore, marched and besieged both these Hill Forts, and after a siege of two months Bahadúr Bundah was taken, it not being a very strong fort. The Commandant of the Fort of Gopul was not however to be deceived by the enemy, and vigourously defended himself, and moreover frequently attacked their batteries, and drove the infidels out of them.

The river, however, still continued to swell to

that degree, that even the basket men, (or water-
men), were unable to cross it, and the passage was
therefore unattainable by the Sultán's troops.   In
consequence, therefore, thirty boats were assembled
from the districts of Hurrihur, Horul (Hurrial),
&c. and three or four hundred large baskets were
also collected, and near two months were expended
in waiting for the decrease of the waters, and even
then, the water, instead of falling, daily rose higher.
The Sultán, therefore, ordered that twenty-one
guns of heavy calibre should be ranged on the
banks of the river, and that ten cartridges should
be fired from each.   The artillery men having executed these orders, from that time the water de-
creased ; and in two or three days fell to half its
former height. The Mahrattas at hearing the report
of the guns, imagining it was a salute for good
news, and that it must be either because a reinforcement of French troops had joined the Sultán's
army, or that the Kuzzaks had made an incursion
into the Hydurabád territory, and had defeated
the Nizám, they therefore determined that to stay
any longer, where they were was unworthy their
military [1] character, and accordingly marched off to
Shanoor, they left, however, ten or twelve thousand
horse, encamped on the bank of the river.

[1] In derision.

When the water had sufficiently subsided, the
Sultán ordered his army to cross over, and first at
night two Kushoons of the Jysh, and two thousand
horse with the artillery, the wind being favourable
were ferried over in boats and immediately fell
upon the Mahratta horse who were entirely unpre-
pared for their arrival, and with sword and musket
drove the dust of existence out of their bodies, and
seven hundred horses with the flag elephant, and a
number of camel drums [m] were taken on this occasion. Those of the Mahrattas who escaped, leaving their horses, arms, and property behind them,
fled towards the main body of their own army, and
informed their chief of the passage of the river
by the Sultán's troops. The next day, therefore,
the Sultán himself with his army of heroes crossed
over the river and pitched his tents on the opposite
bank, where he covered the front of his army
with redoubts, and halted there for the space
of a month; — during this period, the provision,
treasure, artillery and indeed all the departments
with the followers, &c. had crossed over, and the
enemy also, with the design to attack the Sultán,
advanced with their troops and artillery, and encamped four fursungs distant.

In a few days, therefore, the Sultán (the de-

[m] Kettle drums carried on camels.

stroyer of his enemies) with the whole of his horse,
four Kushoons and his guns and stores, left his
encampment, intending to try the strength of his
enemies, and advancing towards them two fursungs,
formed in order on the plain. The Mahrattas
being informed of this movement turned out in
good order, and also formed in order of battle.
The Sipahdárs of the Sultán's cavalry according
to his orders on seeing the approach of the enemy,
posted a body of infantry in the low grounds,
the guns attached to them being loaded with
grape, were kept in readiness, while the household
cavalry accompanied by the horse of the Paigahs,
and the body guard, with great shew paraded
over the higher ground. The Surkheils or commanding officers of the Bede, or irregular horse ;
that is to say, Ghází Khán, Wuli Muhammad,
Ibrahim Khán, &c. agreeably to the Sultán's orders,
formed their lines to the front and advanced to attack the Mahrattas, when, however, the Mahrattas
charged them in turn and they were within arms
length of each other, the Kuzzaks very bravely after
their mode, wheeled off from the flank, and retired
towards their own army. The infidels fully armed
and equipped, now, therefore, pursued them without any consideration or apprehension, and suddenly presented themselves to the muzzles of the

guns.ⁿ The infantry in ambush, therefore, now
immediately rose and advanced, and with the fire
of their guns and musketry, soon took off the
edge of their enemies valour ; and the horse
charging them from the rear raised the clamour
of the day of judgement, until the troops of Islám
and the infidels were mixed and confounded
among each other like light and darkness. Whatever of manhood and courage, therefore, existed
in them was now brought forth, and in the heat
and press of the battle, the rocketeers having
lighted their rockets, threw confusion and dispersion into the masses of the Mahrattas, and the
artillery men from the flank of the line by a continual fire from their guns, scattered their ranks
like as the leaves of trees are scattered by the cold
blasts of autumn. The officers of the Mahrattas,
seeing the signs of defeat and the indications of
flight and dispersion on the foreheads of their
dispirited soldiery, immediately fled, and the victorious army pursued them to the distance of
two fursungs (about seven miles), and crowds of
these dark minded infidels were slain and taken
prisoners.

The Sultán after this victory, marched on and
encamped his victorious army at the distance of

ⁿ Hydur Alí's old manœuvre.

four measured fursungs, in an open and extensive
plain. The plan of the encampment of the conquering army on that day was as follows. — The
Kushoons with their guns were drawn up as a fort,
or in square, (on the flanks, front and rear), and
in the centre were the Sultán's tents and those of
the Durbar, (this I think shews that even after his
victory, the Sultán was afraid of the Mahrattas),
on the right were posted the regiments and Dus-
tahs of cavalry, and on the left the Sillahdár and
Kuzzak horse ; surrounding the Sultán's tents and
Durbar, the infantry called Assud Ilahi, and Ahmudi were stationed. The rear guard was composed of the Ahshám and Gundehchar° infantry,
also the pioneers, Komatties, (Palankin and Dooli
bearers,) and the contingent troops of the Poligars
&c. The horse of the advanced posts, or the
grand guards, were stationed one fursung distant
to furnish videttes.

The enemy likewise with their troops, now got
themselves ready, and advanced to the river of
the town of Kudduk, with the intention to give
battle. The Sultán, therefore, after the lapse of
four or five days, one night formed his Kushoons
under Shaikh Imám, Shaikh Omur, and Imám

° I do not know what description of troops is meant under
this name.

Khán, Sipahdárs, with the guns and rocketeers, and
Ghází Khán, with two thousand horse under
the command of Hussein Alí Khán, Bukhshi, and
Maha Mirza Khán, with an intention to make a
night attack on the Mahrattas, and they were
marched off towards the Mahratta camp, while the
Sultán himself, remained in the centre of his camp
with the Paigah horse, and the rest of the cavalry.

The Sipahdárs and Bukhshees, therefore, proceeding by the road pointed out by the guides,
marched on, and at about four o'clock in the morning, arrived near the Mahratta camp. They had,
however, mistaken the road, and now fell in with
the pickets of the enemy, who had lighted fires here
and there about their posts, and Shaikh Omur who
was with the leading division, seeing these, and
fancying also he saw before him the lines of the
Mahratta army, without informing the other officers of his intention, opened a fire from his guns and
rockets. The report of the guns, rockets &c., soon
awakened the Mahrattas, and some sought the
road of safety, and some of the Mahratta chiefs
attacked the assailants. The Bukhshees of the
Sultán's troops, however, being experienced men,
now quickly wheeled about, and under the cover
of the hills and jungles, avoided their enemies and
returned to the presence, and reported to the

Sultán the whole of the circumstances. The Sultán exceedingly angry at the failure of the expedition, immediately dismissed from his service Shaikh Omur, and gave his Kushoon to a man named Fazil Khán, a Risaldár. The Sultán next day marched and encamped on the river Bola, and the Mahrattas also at the same time changed ground, and encamped at the distance of about nine miles, with their rear resting on a thick jungle. Two days after the Sipahdárs or commandants of regiments or brigades, Imám Khán, Fazil Khán, and Mír Mahmood, with two thousand Kuzzak horse, and one thousand rocketeers, under the command of Kudr Khán, the son of Gházi Khán, were again despatched at night to surprise and plunder the camp of the Mahrattas. The able and experienced Sipahdárs having clothed all their men in Kumlees (a kind of blanket mostly of a black colour) they wound their devious way, like a black snake through the turnings and windings of the hilly road.

After undergoing the labours and fatigues of a long march, they at length arrived in the rear of the Mahratta camp, and when the pickets of the Mahrattas aware of their arrival prepared to oppose them, they in the Mahratta language gave themselves out to be a detachment from the Mo-

ghul (Hydurabád) army sent to their aid from Raichore, and without stopping, marched direct into
the midst of their camp, where they raised a terrible storm with their musketry, rockets and keen
swords, and the bands of the order and discipline
of the Mahrattas were broken asunder, and on all
sides the field of battle was straightened on these
infidels. The chiefs of their army, however, with
the cavalry, jumping on the backs of their horses
without saddles or clothes, fled towards their
park of artillery, which was at a considerable distance.

The able Sipahdárs,[*] victorious, with much plunder, both in money, valuables, arms, and fifteen
hundred mares, having also taken prisoners many
women and children belonging to the Mahratta
chiefs, returned to the presence, and in reward
for their labours were honoured with presents
of jewelled gorgets, strings of pearl, and gold and
silver armlets. The Sultán, however, the emblem
of mercy, despatched the women taken prisoners
with presents of honorary dresses and robes, in
palankins, and under charge of a party of rocketeers
to the Mahratta camp. The Sultán also secretly
despatched four elephants, and eight beautiful
horses, with a sum of money to Hurri Punt, Rastia

[*] The Sipahdárs commanded a brigade or Kushoon.

I

and Madhooba Bini, through the medium of these ladies, and thereby made them the slaves of his commands and munificence.

But to return;—the Mahrattas left their ground where they then were and marched to Sirhutti, where they encamped.

CHAPTER IX.

The retrograde movement made by the Sultán, from motives of policy or convenience, and the pursuit of the Mahrattas ; — also the arrival of Boorhanuddín Sipahsalar, with his troops and the arrival of a convoy of provisions from Nuggur in charge of Budruzzumán Khán Foujdár; also the seizure of the district of Sanore, and the flight of Hukím Khán, and a description of the battles fought between the Infidels and Moslems in the same year 1199, Hijri. — A. D. 1784.

THE Sultán after the night attack made a night march, and the next morning pitched his camp in the Jungle where he remained the whole day. The next night he again marched to the junction of the river Bala with the river Tungbhudra, and there encamped.

It is not to be concealed here, that the cause of these night marches was this ; — from the filth accumulated from the great numbers of horses and bullocks in camp, and from the carcases and stench of those which died, and the multitude of people in camp, flies were generated in such numbers, that they became a pest to the whole army, to such a degree that the soldiers at night even, could neither cook nor eat their victuals ; the Sultán,

therefore, gave orders that they should dissolve
sugar and sweetmeats in water and sprinkle it before their tents, and this being done, when the flies
settled upon this sugar and water, he marched off
and left the ground. At this time Boorhanuddín
Sipahsalar with his division of troops, arrived from
the neighbourhood of Anooti, and Budruzzumán
Khán with an immense convoy of provisions also arrived from the district of Nuggur, and was admitted
to the honour of an audience. When, however,
intelligence of these night marches reached the
Mahrattas, they immediately fancied that they arose
from fear of their mighty army, and that the Sultán
was returning to his capital, and that he had no
power any longer to withstand them ; — they,
therefore, with the whole of their force followed
quickly and encamped at the distance of two fursungs in the rear of the victorious army, so near
that the pickets and outposts of both armies were
stationed at the distance of an arrow's cast only
from each other, and at this distance repelled the
different attacks made by each other.   The Sultán,
therefore, having formed his plans, morning and
evening had his Kushoons out in the plain, under
pretence of exercise,⁴ manœuvring about and firing

⁴ This is one of the stratagems recommended in the Futtah il
Mujahiddín.

from daylight in the morning to eight o'clock; and in the evening from five until it was dark;— and this was done continually. After manœuvring five or six days after this fashion, the Sultán one evening, leaving the baggage and followers of his army in the same place, gave orders to his Amírs, to make a night attack from different points in the mode following:— Mír Moinuddín with two Kushoons, five guns and the French regiment was ordered to attack the right flank of the enemy, and Boorhanuddín with two or three Kushoons and six guns marched towards the left wing of the enemy for the same purpose, while the Sultán himself with two Kushoons, the horse of his Paigah, and the Ahshám foot, advanced with a determination to attack the main body of the enemy.

The night was, however, without moonlight, and so excessively dark, that the troops with the greatest difficulty and labour made their way to the points of attack.* By the light of the false or earliest morning, however, Boorhanuddín, first among them all, attacked the troops of Hurri Punt and Rastia, and opened the gate of dismay and calamity upon them; Mír Moinuddín, embarrassed by his guns, which, owing to the deep mud of the roads could not be got on, left them behind,

صبح کاذب ٢

and with two light French guns marching quick fell
upon the troops of Syfe Jung, (in some copies he
is called Subkut Jung') or, the right wing of the
Nizám's army, (the symbol of flight) which was
entirely unsuspicious of such tricks of the night,'
and caused the confusion of the day of judgment
to fall among them.

At this time, the Sultán himself with the greatest
rapidity moved on to attack the main body of the
enemy.   These attacks on all sides having com-
pressed the Mahrattas in a small space, the chiefs
of that army, who were bound to the service of the
Sultán, keeping aloof from the action, the Moghul
army was entirely overrun and plundered, and all
their baggage and property trodden under the hoofs
of the Sultán's horse.   For the rest, the chiefs of
the Mahrattas mounting their horses fled to the
Tope Khána, or park of artillery, which was about
one fursung distant.   The baggage of the army
and the stores and wealth of the Oordoo Bazar of
the Mahrattas, fell, therefore, into the possession
of the servants of the Sultán, and the tents, camels,
standards and horses with their head and heel ropes,
&c. were all taken.   The Sultán remained to rest
and refresh his troops the whole day in the Mahratta camp ; after mid-day, however, the troops of

سبقة جنگ '   بازي شب '

the Mahrattas assembled and advanced with their
heaviest guns, about a fursung, and, taking possession ᵘ of some high ground, placed them in battery there, and opened their fire with such pre-
cision, that they greatly distressed the Sultán's
army, and broke the arms and legs of many of his
soldiers.

The Sultán's anger now flamed violently at the
insolence of the Mahrattas, and he ordered that
they should be driven from their position, and Syud
Hamíd, Shaíkh Onsur, and Ahmud Beg, Sipahdárs,
therefore, with the regiments of Monsieur Lally,
marched, following the low grounds to attack the
Mahratta park of artillery; — it happened, however, that on their way thither, they fell in with a
large body of the Mahrattas; estimated at thirty
thousand well appointed horse, who had concealed
themselves in the dry bed of a tank ˣ near their
position, and were lying in wait for an opportunity
to attack the Sultán's troops. The brave Sipahdárs and gallant Frenchmen immediately levelled
their muskets and poured forth their fire in vollies
with such effect, that the enemy from the tumult
and throng, could not wheel about without difficulty, and, therefore, of necessity presented their
breasts as a mark for the bullets and bayonets of

ᵘ A mistake here.   ˣ It must have been a large tank.

the musketeers, and they were consequently pierced
with as many holes as a net; two officers of the
Mahrattas, who each rode an elephant, were killed,
and the rest leaving their horses and arms escaped
with their lives only. In fine, in the twinkling of
an eye, seven or eight thousand horse of the Mahrattas were destroyed and their bodies scattered
upon the plain.

When the chief of the Mahrattas saw the marks
of fear and despondency on the foreheads of his
soldiers, he turned away from the fight, and his
courage failing him, he withdrew his guns and retreated to the distance of two stages. The Sultán,
now therefore victorious, with the spoil of the
Mahrattas, his drums beating for joy at his success, returned to his tent, and the next day marched
further on towards Sanore.

It is not to be omitted here, that Abdul Hukím
Khán, the chief of that state, after the death of the
Nawáb, without reason estranged his heart from the
Sultán, indeed from his (the Sultán's) youth even,
he had been his inveterate enemy : — moreover
after the accession of the Sultán, he sent neither
letters of congratulation, nor presents of cloths,
&c., courtesies which are esteemed the pledges of
friendship and good-will. His agent, however,
Chíntoo Pundit, on his own part, and merely to

pay court to the Sultán, made some presents, but
although these circumstances hurt and aggrieved
the feelings of the Sultán ;— still on account of
the ties of relationship which existed between
them, the Sultán gave him no molestation, but
on the contrary, overlooked some very unworthy
actions done by him.

Notwithstanding all this, this unlucky man never
put any confidence in the Sultán, and had now
leagued and intrigued with the Mahrattas.   When
he found, therefore, that the Sultán was approach-
ing him, reflecting on his own unworthy conduct,
he trembled like a reed at the sound of the hoofs
of the Sultán's horse, and with certain of his friends,
and the dependents of his household, that is his
women and a small sum of money he had by him,
he at night fled and joined the army of the Mahrattas, leaving Abdul Khira Khán, alias Khira Mean
in the city.   The date of this flight is given in the
following Hindostanni words,

' حکیم خان میانه سب کو چهورکی اب بهاگا

When the Sultán heard of his flight, and his junction with the Mahrattas, he was astonished, but at
night despatched Syud Humíd, and Syud Ghuffar
Sipahdárs to take possession of the city, and in the
morning he himself marched and encamped before

' Hakím Khán Meeana, left all and ran away.

the place, and then despatched Mír Sadik, and Mahdi
Khán, Bukhshi, with orders that all the property
and wealth of the state of Sanore, which the Kháns
of former days had collected at a vast expense,
should be sent to the presence, and all this Hukím
Khán by his foolish enmity gave gratuitously to the
winds. The officers sent, agreeably to their orders,
without opposition from any one, took and despatched to the presence whatever they found of
gold, silver, carpets, or tents, vessels, arms, &c. ;
as for instance, in Abdul Hukím's wardrobe, they
found fifty turbans of different colours, of the
Boorhanpoor chintz kind, hung upon pegs in the
wall, and honorary dresses of great splendour and
value, of the same colour corresponding to the
turbans, under cloth covers or in packages : — but
besides these, articles of great value brought from
all countries laid about in heaps, and these with
lists of all of them were sent to the Sultán, and
after being inspected by him were deposited in the
Tosha Khána.

The light guns were all added to the Sultán's
artillery, and one gun composed of five metals, *
twelve legal guz in length was broken up and sent
to the mint to be coined into halfpence. In fact,
all the valuables, among which were carpets of the

پنج رس *

most elegant patterns with gold and silver flowers, each the load of four or five camels, and the Kalecchas and Sutrinjas, (other kinds of carpets) of which each was the load of an elephant, were all seized by the Sultán's servants. A short time after this, Khira Mean on horseback, and accompanied by two or three servants arrived, and was honoured by being admitted to an audience ; — at this audience the Sultán addressed him and said, "what has befallen your father, that he should have run away in this manner? we ourselves in no matter, and in no mode, ever interfered with or molested him, but on the contrary, our favour towards him increased daily; but setting this aside, shame on your relationship, that without any injury or breach of engagement on our part, your father should have joined with the Mahrattas, the enemies of our house and openly displayed his hostility. Depend on it that he will never be the better for it, nor ever see the days of prosperity." Khira Mean in reply, said, " that undoubtedly his father had acted unwisely, and that the bread of his fortunes had been dried up in the sun of despair ; — that he, the Sultán's ransom, or sacrifice, was ignorant of what had been done, or he would have opposed it to the utmost of his power." After this the Sultán placed him near his own tent, and sent him twice a day, dishes from his own table; — he, however, kept him under strict restraint or surveillance in the same way that he kept Kumruddín.

125

CHAPTER X.

An account of another night attack, the last battle and the
defeat of the Mahrattas by the victorious army, and the establishment of Peace between the Lion conquering the world, the Sultán
and his weak incompetent enemies the Mahrattas; also the regulation of the districts of the Poligars, with other events which
occurred in the year 1200, Hijri. — A. D. 1785-6.

THE Sultán after the capture and regulation of
Sanore, leaving a garrison in that city, marched
to the northward, and encamped near Jobun Gurh,
and halted there for thirteen days of the month
Mohurrum il Huram. He now also distributed
his army into four divisions; each consisting of
four Kushoons, five thousand irregular foot, five
thousand Silladár horse,* and fifteen guns. The
first division was placed under the command of
Mír Moinuddín, otherwise called Syud Sáhib; —
the second division was placed under Boorhanuddín; — the third was committed to the charge
of Maha Mirza Khán; and the fourth to Hussein
Alí Khán, the Mír Bukhshi.

Having done this, the Sultán ordered them to

خودداسپه *

march on, and directed that the aforesaid divisions should encamp at the distance of three miles from the remainder of his army. The Sipahsalars, therefore, in obedience to these orders, took up their ground, and employed themselves in preparing their troops and arms for immediate action, — while the Sultán himself with two Kushoons, the Assud Ilahi and Ahmudi; three Mokubs or regiments of horse, eight Dustas [b] of the Paigah, or household horse, four thousand Kuzzaks and ten thousand Ahshám infantry, remained encamped where he was. On these arrangements, it was currently reported by him, that of the Sipahsalars, (the officers commanding these divisions,) the first was commissioned to the conquests of the dependencies of Hydurabad; the second to the conquest of those of Poona; the third to the maintenance of order at Raichore, Kottoor, &c.; and the fourth to the capital, Puttun, to subject and controul the different forts and districts of the Poligars, — while the Sultán himself was to attack the Mahrattas. The commander of the Mahratta army at hearing this news, became like quicksilver, restless and uneasy, when of a sudden, Mír Moinuddín, with his force, at the instance of Syud Humíd, and Syud Ghuffar, marched at night and attacked the hill

[b] A Dusta was about twelve hundred, in Tipú's army.

fort of Mondergi Droog, which was garrisoned by
the Mahrattas, — and at one assault took the fort
and passed the garrison under the edge of the
sword. The town was also pillaged, and he returned with stores of provisions and much gold and
jewels. In the same way Boorhanuddín marched
towards Binkapoor and Misri Kote, which were in
the occupation of the Mahrattas, in a way that no
one could be aware of his arrival, and unfurling
the standard of enterprize, carried exceeding terror and dismay among them, and lighted up the
fire of plunder and slaughter in all that quarter.
The Sultán also now advanced straight towards
the enemy, the sign or symbol of defeat.[c] In
that march, however, the Mahrattas attacked the
rear-guard of the victorious army, and brought a
storm of evil on its followers, and plundered the
Banjaras of ten thousand bags of grain, which
they carried off. The Sultán now, therefore,
despatched a message to the Commander of the
Mahratta forces to this effect, that it was unworthy of noble generous minds to injure or distress God's people without cause, and, that if he
(the Mahratta) had the breath of manhood still
remaining in him, their dispute might be settled in

[c] In contra-distinction, the Sultan's army being invariably the
victorious army.

an hour, that his wish was, that in a well fought
battle of one day, they should finish the book of
strife and contention. As the chief of the Mahrattas well knew the valour, (meaning the reverse)
of his own troops, and that without peace, he could
not expect to save himself from destruction, he
declined to agree to the Sultán's proposition. However, by the advice of certain of his servants, who
recommended war, he agreed to an action to be decided with the sword alone. The Sultán, therefore,
one day assembled his four divisions on the river
Guduk, and arranged them in order of battle, and,
having appointed his Kushoons to the right and left
wings, he himself mounted on an elephant with his
guard, took his station on the field, and first
ordered the brave men of his Paigah, or household cavalry, to commence the action, and accordingly each Dusta galloped forward, and having
formed in close order took possession of the field.[d]
The Mahrattas also armed cap-a-piè, now charged
the Sultán's troops, and between them a very
severe action ensued. It was, however, determined, that each Dusta should fight only half an
hour, that the devotion and bravery of the whole

[d] I should have attempted a description of Tipú's military
regulations from the Futtah ul Mujahiddín, and other works, but
there is not sufficient interest in such details to repay the trouble.

army, officers, and men, might be fairly tested.
Every brave man, therefore, made the utmost display
of his courage, and many by their prowess effaced
the renown of the great actions of Roostum and
Isfendiar, and until mid-day, the clashing of swords,
the whistling of arrows, and the rustling of the
spears * continued so great and so constant, that
the gallant troopers at length quitted their swords
and spears, and laying hands on each other had
recourse to their poignards and daggers, and on
every side lay heaps of slain.   After the brave men
of the Paigah, the Silladárs, next stretching forth
the arms of manhood, made the face of the plain
as red as the rosy morn, with the blood of their
enemies.   The chiefs of the Mahrattas, however,
aware they were not able to resist the swords of
the worshippers of fame, in the pride of superior
numbers determined to charge with their whole
force, and thus ride over the Sultán's army, and
accordingly with this intention, they with all their
troops, amounting to seventy or eighty thousand
men, moved forward.   The Sultán, now seeing
that the Mahrattas had violated their agreement,

---

* The noise made by the strokes or cuts of the sword, is represented by the word شِبَاشِب ; that made by the striking or
whistling of an arrow, جِقَاجِق and that made by the piercing
of a spear, كُهِبَاكُهِب .

immediately gave orders to his artillery, and they
moving forward quickly from the flanks with the
Sipahdárs (and their Kushoons) by their heavy fire of
musketry and artillery, soon compelled the unfortunate Mahrattas to taste the sherbet of flight. As
soon, therefore, as they were scattered and dispersed, the regiments of horse, and the Kuzzaks,
of the victorious army followed them for two fursungs, and took from them to the amount of two
or three thousand horses, a quantity of baggage,
stores and arms ; as arrows, swords, and two pieces
of cannon, and then returned. The Mahrattas on
the contrary, for three stages never looked behind
them and fled without halting even for the night.
Hurri Náík the Poligar of Kunuk Giri, who at first
had attached himself to the Mahrattas, seeing at
this time the irregularity of their measures and
movements, now finding an opportunity, left them
with his troops and offered his services to the Sultán, who received him with great favour.

The Sultán after this marched with his army to
Binkapoor, and encamped eighteen kose to the northward of Sanore : — at this place a party of Kuzzak
horse left the army with an intention to plunder
the villages in that vicinity. It so happened, however, that the outposts of the Mahrattas obtained in
formation of this movement, and posted themselves

on the road by which they (the Kuzzaks) marched
and at one charge surrounded and killed every
man of them. The Sultán hearing of this was
greatly incensed, and issued orders to the other
Kuzzaks, with his army and to his own horse, that
no one should proceed beyond the limits of the
outposts, or grand guards, without permission. In
this encampment the Sultán remained one month,
and in that time, by dispensing gold and sending
honorary dresses and presents of all kinds in the
way of courtesy and friendship, made several of
the chiefs of the Mahrattas obedient, and the slaves
of his commands, and all operations were undertaken by the advice and instruction of these men,
until one day, when, according to the hints and
directions of these chiefs, all four divisions of the
army were made ready, and marched off for a
night attack, and the Sultán having assembled a
number of hermaphrodites ᶠ belonging to his camp,
to the amount of about one hundred and fifty, he
gave them painted sticks and placed them in front
of each division.

The pickets of the Mahrattas who were the
servants of Hurri Punt Phirkia, seeing and knowing the Sultán's troops, allowed them to pass.
When, however, the Sipahsalars arrived near the

هيزان ᶠ

Mahratta encampment, one of the Mahrattas becoming aware of their approach, apprised Holkar,
that they had entered the camp through the villany and collusion of the officers in command of
the pickets; Holkar, on hearing this, left his tent
on foot, and he had no sooner quitted it than the
fire of the rockets and musketry blazing close to
his eyes, he immediately ran away leaving his
favourite wife asleep in the tent, and the rest of
the Mahratta chiefs followed his example. The
whole of the camp, therefore, after this was plundered, and the half alive Moghul camp, was also
completely pillaged, and eighteen women, the wives
of the Mahratta chiefs, with their gold and jewels
were taken. As soon as the morning dawned
the Sipahsalars, victorious, with the captured baggage of the Mahrattas, their standards, tents, elephants, camels, treasure and four guns, marched
on their return, and notwithstanding the Mahrattas rallied those of their army spared by the
sword, and that they seized and occupied the road
by which the Sultán's troops returned, and fought
desperately to cut them off; — still, it was of no
avail, and they were compelled to retire, and the
Sipahsalars on their arrival were honoured by ad-
mission to the presence, and they presented the
plundered property and the women taken to the

Sultán; the liberal Sultán to every officer and
soldier who had distinguished himself on this occasion, gave two months additional pay, besides other
honours and advantages.

The women taken prisoners were dismissed as
before, after making an agreement, which they
confirmed with solemn oaths to the effect that by
every art and means, they would prevent their
husbands from continuing the war, and that they
would never withdraw their hands from importu-
nity and solicitation, until their husbands laid their
heads in submission on the orders of the Sultán.
On the arrival of the women in the Mahratta camp,
their husbands fearing they had been polluted, and
that the veil of their honour had been rent by the
rude hands of the Mussulmans who made them
prisoners, placed them all in a tent pitched separately for them, and did not allow them to enter
their tents.

The women, therefore, now opened their mouths
to reproach and revile the illiberality and want of
shame manifested by their husbands, to extol their
own purity; to praise the kind and honourable
treatment they had received from the Sultán; and
lastly pertinaciously to insist that peace should be
made.

The chiefs of the Mahrattas, therefore, now

cleared from their minds the bad opinions they
had formed, and discharged from their hearts the
deep rooted enmity in which they had indulged,
but still from a sense of duty exerted themselves
in the execution of the orders of their chief —
however, on whatever side the Sultán's troops advanced to the attack, they as constantly retired; —
When the Sultán, therefore, found there was no
readiness for action on the part of the enemy's
troops, after the lapse of a month, casting the eyes
of compassion on God's people, according to the
hints and instructions of the chiefs of the Mahrattas and Moghul armies, he commenced to set
on foot negotiations for the establishment of peace,
and Budruzzumán Khán and other Kháns, with
friendly letters, a sum of money, some rarities,
valuable cloths and jewels, among which was one
diamond necklace, worth five lakhs⁵ of rupees,
were despatched to Poona.

Holkar and other chiefs of the Mahratta army,
who had been often defeated by the Sultán's troops,
and whose women and wealth had been so often
pillaged and violated by them, now reduced to
extremities, detailed the bravery and enterprize of
the Sultán's army in their letters to Poona, and
strenuously advocated the conclusion of peace.

⁵ 500,000.

When the chief of Poona, (the Paishwa) and his
minister consulted with their chief officers,[b] on
this measure, the latter said, our best policy apparently is, that we should also send embassadors
with rarities and presents to the Sultán, and thereby
wash the dust of enmity from off his offended
mind with the pure water of conciliation, and refresh and revive the garden of our territories with
the flowing stream of amity and concord ; for this
reason that the impression and effect of an asso-
ciation with the Mussulmàn King, would be the
source of order and strength to our state, and even
if it were not so, that the character for courage and
prowess of that great man the Sultán, was so well
known, that should he turn the reins of his operations to our quarter, he would inevitably conquer
the whole of our country, and the hereditary possessions of the Mahratta empire, would be taken
out of the hands of their race. As these words of
advice took effect on the hearts of the chiefs and
as they had also heard that a body of French
troops had arrived to the aid of the Sultán, the
offer of negotiation on his part was considered by
them as a most fortunate occurrence, and they
accepted the embassadors and presents and the
dust of enmity existing on both sides was washed

کارپرداز[b]

off by the water of friendship, and they also despatched an embassador with presents of rarities,
honorary dresses, gold, jewels, fine horses and
elephants to the presence of the conquering Sultán.

They requested, however, that the Talookas of
Nargoonda, Nolegoonda, and Jalihul should be
presented to them as gifts. The Sultán, the
asylum of the world, from policy and according to
the *verse*, — " be generous, be generous that the
stranger may become thy slave," — agreed to their
request, and forwarded the Sunnuds of those three
Talookas to them. It is not to be omitted here,
that as the chief of Poona (the Paishwa) gave the
Sultán's embassadors the district of Kuslupoor in
Jageer, so that in return, the Sultán gave him these
three Talookas.

The forts and towns in that neighbourhood which
by the neglect and villany of traitors, had fallen
into the possession of the troops of the enemy,
were now restored to the Sirkar Khodádád — included in these negotiations was the petition of
Hurri Punt for the pardon of all the offences,
great and small, of Hukím Khán, which was obtained by his mediation, and the Souba of Sanore
was again restored to him as before. When the
Sultán's mind on the score of peace was fully satis-

fied and at rest, he returned victorious to the town
of Sanore. Hurri Punt Phirkia who had placed
the ring of obedience in the ear of his existence,
and who was the origin and founder of the peace,
had the Talooka of Gujindur Gurb, with its dependencies, and several towns of Kunchun Gurh,
presented to him in Jageer to furnish his Paun
and Betel nut expenses.[1] The Sultán then marched
on by the route of Gopul and Bahadúr Bundah,
and crossing the river (Tungbhudra) encamped
on the tank of the Duroojee Muhl, which lies two
kose to the eastward of Anagoondi, and in order
to complete the repairs of this tank, halted there
some time. During this period, the Poligars of
Rai Droog and Hurpun Hulli, accompanied by a
number of their dependents, entered the Sultán's
camp in the hope of being admitted to an audience. The Sultán, however, bore a violent hatred
to these chiefs for this reason, that whenever they
were summoned, they declined to attend, owing
to their ill will towards him, and therefore, all wish
to accept their services, or admit them, was totally
rejected from his mind.

He at night, therefore, despatched his Kushoons
and making prisoners of them and their depen-

[1] Paun is a leaf eaten with Betel nut, well known in India;
called by the natives Tamul Puttra.

dents, put them in irons and sent them prisoners to Bangalore, [k] and all their territory, wealth and property of all kinds were seized, and their districts and forts assigned to able civil officers, and brave military governors, a brother of the chief of Hurpun Hulli, however, who was residing in some town of that district in ill health, when he saw the torrent of the Sultán's anger and the waters of calamity surrounding him, fled at night with his wife, family and dependents, and leaving the latter at Dumul proceeded to Mirch, and he, therefore, escaped with his life and property. The Sultán after this marched and entered his capital, Seringaputtun.

[k] One died at Seringaputtun, and the other was poisoned by Tipú, according to Col. Marriott.

CHAPTER XI.

An account of the re-establishment of order in the City of Seringaputtun, the regulation of the whole of the Sultán's territories and the dismission from office of Mír Sadik, Dewán, or Minister of state, also, the completion of the Alí Musjid, — the return of the Embassadors from the presence of the Sultán of Room, or Constantinople, sent thither in the year 1198 Hijri : — and the despatch of an Embassador to Hydurabád with other events of the year 1202, Hijri, — A. D. 1787.

WHEN the capital of the kingdom was enlightened by the resplendent countenance of the Sultán, the dispenser of justice, his world conquering mind occupied itself in the regulation of his kingdom and army. At this time also the exactions and tyranny of the Dewán, or minister of state (Mír Sadik) who according to his caprice and will oppressed·the people of the Souba of Adhooni and Sanoor, having been represented to the Sultán his services were dispensed with, that is he was dismissed; the property in his house being seized according to orders, two lakhs of rupees the currency of Adhooni, which is called Chulaoni, and one lakh of hoons or pagodas, Muhammad Sháhi, were found, and he was put in irons and imprisoned,

and Mehdi Khán, Nayut, the Jageerdár of Awul-
goonda, was appointed to the Dewáni (in his place).
At this time the Sultán determined to recommence
the building of the Musjidi Ala, the erection of which
had been suspended since the year 1198 Hijri, and
the Daroghu of public buildings, according to the
plan, which will be mentioned hereafter, completed
it in two years, at the expense of three lakhs of
rupees, and the prayers of the Eedi Fitr, in the
year 1204, Hijri, were the first said in that mosque,
and it was named by the Sultán Musjidi Ala.

A concise account of the cause of the building
this Mosque is as follows : — it is, known, that
when the vile and rejected Brahman Khunda Rao,
with the intention of uprooting the fortunes of
his Master, began to excite disturbances, and the
late Nawáb fled alone to Bangalore, and that villain imprisoned the Nawáb's Zunana and the Sultán
(who was then a boy of six or seven years of age,)
in a house in the fort, near the gate of the Deorai
Peenth, which at present is called the Gunjam
gate : — at that period, before this house, there
stood a Hindu temple, the area or space round
which was large. The Sultán, therefore, in his
infancy being like all children, fond of play, and as
in that space boys of the Kinhiri and Brahman
castes assembled to amuse themselves, was accus-

tomed to quit the house to see them play, or play
with them. It happened one day during this
period, that a Fakír (a religious mendicant) a man
of saint-like mind passed that way, and seeing the
Sultán gave him a life bestowing benediction, saying to him, " Fortunate child, at a future time thou
wilt be the king of this country, and when that
time comes, remember my words ; — take this
temple and destroy it, and build a Musjid in its
place, and for ages it will remain a memorial of
thee." The Sultán smiled, and in reply told him,
" that whenever, by his blessing, he should become
a Padisháh, or king, he would do as he (the Fakír)
directed." When, therefore, after a short time his
father became a prince, the possessor of wealth
and territory, he remembered his promise, and
after his return from Nuggur and Gorial Bundur,
he purchased the temple from the adorers of the
image in it (which after all was nothing but the
figure of a bull, made of brick and mortar) with
their goodwill, and the Brahmans, therefore, taking
away their image, placed it in the Deorai Peenth,
and the temple was pulled down, and the foundations
of a new Musjid raised on the site, agreeably to a
plan of the Mosque, built by Alí Adil Sháh, at
Bejapoor, and brought from thence.

As, however, the regulation of the kingdom, the

chastisement of the rebellious, such as the people
of Koorg, the Mahrattas and the Poligars were
the first objects in the mind of the late Nawáb,—
the work fell into delay for a time, but now, when
from the blessing of God all these difficulties had
been removed, the work was resumed.

The Sultán now divided the whole of the territory under his authority into three parts, each of
which he distinguished by a different name; as
for instance, the country on the coast was called
the Souba Yum, (the sea); the cities and towns
of the hilly and woody country, the Souba
Turun;—and the open and level or champaign
country, the Souba Ghubra (the earth). The
chief officers of Purgunas also received the title of
Asof. About this time also, round every city,
town and fort, at the distance of one fursung, he
erected a strong stockade with four gates, and to
these he appointed vigilant guards, that no one
without his authority and permission, and the
signature or mark of the military governor should
be permitted to pass in or out. By this restric-
tion, therefore, the intercourse of foreign merchants and the commercial men of the country
was entirely cut off; the reason of this was that
the deceased Nawáb had collected Muhammadans
from all countries, and had filled his kingdom

with them contrary to its former state (when it
was full of Hindoos). When these people, therefore, by the gifts, presents and liberality of the
Nawáb and of the kind hearted Sultán became rich
in gold and other valuables, they without leave or
licence departed and returned to their own countries. These restrictions were intended, therefore,
to prevent their doing so in future. In addition
to this, the Sultán stockaded the frontier between
the limit of his dominions and the districts of the
Karnatic Payanghaut, from the boundaries of Dindigul and Kuroor, to the Ghaut or Mountains of
Budweil, and the limits of Khumum, and twelve
thousand foot soldiers were stationed along this
stockade, as a cordon, in order to prevent any one
from entering his dominions from the Payanghaut,
or any one from quitting the Balu Ghaut for that
quarter.

The silver coins and rupees called Imámi,
having on one side the misra or line, " The religion
of Ahmud enlightened the world from the victories
of Hydur;"[1] and on the reverse the sentence, " He
is the sole or only just King,"[h] were coined by his
orders.

The institution of the Muhammadi year which is

دین احمد در جهان روشن زفتح حیدر است ۱

هو السلطان الوحید العادل ۲

thirteen years more than, or exceeding that of the
Hijri, it being reckoned from the conclusion of the
prophet's office, and the commencement of the duties
of his mission (the office of prophet and that of a particular mission are considered distinct) being previously arranged and ready, was now made current
throughout the whole extent of the Sultán's dominions. In this year Gholám Alí Khán, Nuhnoo
Mean and others, who in the year 1198, Hijri, were
sent to the Sultán of Room (Constantinople), with
presents, worthy of the two Sultáns, such as new
muskets, fabricated in the Sultán's arsenal, ten
lakhs of rupees newly coined, valuable cloths, with
gold and jewels, of great value, selected from all
the departments of the state ;ᵃ now returned from
thence having fully obtained the objects of their mission, with a sword and shield, ornamented with
jewels, and friendly and congratulatory letters from
the Vuzírs or ministers of the foot of the Mussulman
Throne, (the Sultán of Room is apparently considered the head of the Muhammadan powers or
states)ᵇ and having presented themselves to the

ᵃ Treasury, wardrobe and Zunana.
ᵇ In the war against Tipú Sultán, in the Mysore, evidence has
appeared of letters to the Ottoman Porte, claiming his aid as the
" Head of the Moslem world," and Mahmood appears fully sen-
sible of the hold which this rank invests him with over his most
powerful vassals. — Upham's Ottoman Empire, Vol. I.

Sultán, they there detailed the circumstances of
their mission, stating that the presents sent (to
Constantinople) were all approved and accepted,
but that among the warlike weapons none were so
much esteemed and admired by the Sultán of
Room as the rockets of which there were none in
that country. The Sultán now, therefore, according to the suggestions of the Vuzírs of Room, and
the advice of his faithful Amírs, collected all the
treasures of the state, or rather assumed the pomp
and splendour of royalty,[p] and directed the formation of a throne of gold, ornamented with jewels
of great value in the shape of a tiger, a figure
from the first most approved by the Sultán.
English and French artisans, also of the greatest
talents were assembled and constantly employed
in casting metal or brass guns [q] and the manufac-
ture of muskets; they also made scissors, pen-
knives, hour-glasses, pocket-knives with many
blades, &c. so that in the course of a month, one
gun and five or six muskets of the best kinds were
completed. The Sultán's manufactories were called
Tara Mundul[r] and were established in four places,

---

[p] It appears from this that Tipú wanted the sanction of the
Sultán of Room, before he assumed the titles and distinctions of
royalty.   [q] بَنْدُوق

[r] Signifying a constellation.

one in the Capital, another at Bangalore, the third
at Chitul Droog, and the fourth at Nuggur; the
chief part of the Sultán's time was, however, spent
in collecting and enlisting men for his horse and
foot, but notwithstanding this, the Amírs and Kháns
of old times, whom the late Nawáb had allured to
his service from all cities and countries, at the expense of hundreds of thousands of pounds, were
now all at once cast down from rank and power,
and the honour of the Sultán's confidence; and low
bred, vulgar, young men were appointed in their
places. The Karwan Bashiaun, that is the chief
merchants and horse-dealers, &c. on account of
low prices or the want of demand for their goods,
abandoned trade and those persons who were
willing to take up a musket and a pair of pistols
were entered in the cavalry, and those who opposed this innovation were deprived of their rank
and dismissed. As the confidence of the Sultán
was chiefly placed in artillery and muskets, as the
most efficient descriptions of arms, the brave men
who excelled at* the handling of the sword and spear
lost heart, and some cavalry officers were appointed
and compelled to enlist men for the Jysh and Uskur
horse and foot, who were ignorant of the rules and
qualifications necessary for these divisions of the

* Le maniement des armes blanches.

service, and consequently in a short time, confusion
and ruin appeared in the fundamental regulations
of the government and kingdom. About this time
Kotubuddín Khán, Dowlut Zai, Alí Ruza, called
Arkati, and Muhammad Ghiaus, companions and
friends of the Sultán and his Amírs were despatched as embassadors to Hydurabád with valua-
able presents and friendly letters, the object of
which was to strengthen the foundations of concord and amity, and that each should aid and support the other in all territorial and fiscal measures,
and also to strengthen these relations by the ties
of kindred and marriage, purely with regard to the
interests of Islám. When the embassadors were
admitted to the honour of an audience by Nizám
Alí Khán, they presented the cloths and valuable
jewels, and in private and in a friendly manner,
represented, that, to the enlightened mind of the
Nizám, it must be evident that rank and greatness
in this world did not possess the quality of dura-
tion, and that its pleasures were always in a state
of change, or evanescence; ᵗ that it was known to
all that the whole of the countries of the Dukkun
and Telingana, was formerly in the powerful grasp
of a fortunate man of the Bahmuni race, and that
from the terror of the sword of that prince, the face

ᵗ A Verse is omitted here.

of the territory of Islám was freed from the thorns
and brambles of infidel opposition. At this time,
therefore, that a Muhammadan Padishah or King
should accord with and make friends of faithless
infidels, and then cause them to lay violent hands
on the territory and wealth of Mussulmans, and
the helpless inhabitants to be burned with the
fire of persecution, would certainly meet reproba-
tion both from God and man, and moreover that
this dishonourable conduct would be the cause
of shame and retribution at the last day; — that
it would be better, therefore, that the dust of enmity and revenge should be allayed by the pure
water of peace and that the military and peace-
able classes should not be disturbed, or their
faith shaken for the enjoyment of pomp and
state a few days; at best a very short time—that
for the sake, of their country and religion they
should fold up the carpet of enmity to each other,
and strengthen the foundations of friendship and
regard, by the rites of matrimonial connexion,
that united in repelling and conquering the infidels, they might so use their best endeavours
that the whole of the Mooslim population, the
poor, the peasantry, and strangers might repose
on the couch of safety and comfort, and pass their
time in prayer for the long continuance of the

reigns of the Kings of Islám. This address from
the able and eloquent embassador, although it
made him (the Nizám) smile like the full blown
rose, yet, as the sentences of the letter included
the mention of matrimonial connexion, he, excited by his folly, became angry and gave these
joy dispensing words no place in his envious mind,
and considering the term Náík which belonged to
the Sultán's forefathers as discreditable, and relationship with him a disgrace, according to the
advice of his foolish women, he turned his face
aside from the true path and dismissed the Eelchi,
or embassador, without the attainment of his object. A detail of the disputes and quarrels which
occurred at the time when Kotubuddín Khán returned is not entered in this book.

It is not to be omitted here, that the Nizám
entertained this vain and absurd opinion, that except
himself, no one of the princes of the Dukkun was
of noble lineage, and on his own nobility and
greatness he gave himself these airs,—did he not
know that the term Náík in the language of the
Rajas of Hind, signifies a chief of courage and
renown? and even omitting this, the Náíkwar
tribe is not distinct from the four tribes; ª—that

* Does he mean the Mooslim, Shaíkh, Syud, Moghul, Puthan,
or is it the Hindu divisions of caste ?

they should be considered low and vulgar. In truth in his birth the Sultán was not in any wise inferior to the others, (that is the Nizám and his family;) he was not born of a low woman, and as for his claim to consideration on the score of wealth, grandeur, state and power, he had a long and powerful arm, and in courage and ability he was unequalled. Some ignorant men who deny the respectability of the surname of his ancestors, have fallen into a great error. Do they not know that the power of the Almighty, the truly and only powerful, is infinite? that he can select any one he pleases and make him great in both worlds, and in this lower world can exalt him to the highest pinnacle of rank and station. It appears as if they knew nothing of the History of Timúr Gorkan Sáhib Kiran (Tamerlane), from whom the powerful dynasty of the emperors of Hind is derived; what was his origin, and what did he become!—It appears also, as if they had never heard of Hussein Kango the first of the Sultáns of the Bhamunia dynasty, and who was styled Hussein Sháh Bhamani, and of whom it is related, that after his death the blazing lightning passed round the enclosure or precinct, (or rather performed the Towwáf[x]) of his tomb, the marks of the passage of which still remain,

طَوَان [x]

and who he was? Good God is it possible that
on the strength of worldly power and distinction,
low fellows boast of their noble descent and men
of the dregs of the people, falsely claim to be
Shaíkhs and Syuds, (the noblest families or tribes
among the Mussulmans) and consider no one equal
to themselves! — *Verse* — " Low birth is hidden
by wealth and station."—" The golden veil con-
ceals the ugliness of the old courtesan."

CHAPTER XII.

The march of the Sultán and his army towards Kalikote, and an account of the attack of Koochi Bundur (Cochin), and the dependencies of the Raja of Maliwar,[7] and the defeat and heavy loss sustained by the victorious army from the mistakes or errors of the guides, and the second attack and conquest of that port, — occurrences of the year 1205, Hijri. — A. D. 1790.

THE conquering Sultán, giving no attention to the tales of the envious and interested, had just completed some private arrangements, when his spies brought intelligence that the Naimars of Kalikote, had placed the foot of insubordination in the path of presumption, and that they had determined to rebel ; that Urshud Beg Khán, the Governor or Foujdár of that district, although he exerted himself to compose or pacify them, and by presents of turbans and shelahs,[*] (ornamental apparel) strove to gain their hearts : — still the infidels were unsettled and restless. The Sultán at hearing of these things ordered the immediate attendance of the Foujdár, and a certain number of the chiefs of the Naimars. The former according to the Sultán's

---

[7] Malabar.   [*] Cloths worn over the shoulders.

orders made himself ready to attend; but the
Naimars under excuses of to-day and to-morrow
refused. At this time a spy, an interested man
and a dire enemy to the Foujdár before mentioned,
represented to the Sultán, that he, the Naimars,
and the Raja of Maliwar, had united in heart and
hand, and that he was sacrificing the interests of
the Sultán for his own emolument and advantage.
In consequence of this, the Sultán with his Amírs
and court, four Kushoons, three Mowkubs or regiments of horse, and his artillery, marched towards
that quarter, secretly determined to extirpate the
rebellious infidels. They, therefore, at the march
of the Sultán, being much alarmed and fearful of
the destruction of themselves and families, dispersed among the woody and mountainous parts of
the country. The Foujdár, however, advanced immediately to meet the Sultán, and having presented himself, was addressed by the Sultán in the
following angry words; — "You were appointed
to the government or regulation of this district, —
what have you done? — You were ordered, moreover, by every art and device to make the Poligar
of Maliwar obedient and tributary, and having collected his Paishkush to despatch it to the presence, — this also has not been done." The Foujdár in reply represented, "Your slave was so

entirely occupied in the subjection of, or keeping in
order the Naimars of this quarter, that he had no
leisure to employ himself in any thing else, — that
independently of this, the Poligar was tributary to
the Souba of the Karnatic, and, therefore, he was
not likely to be deceived by any arts or devices of
his ; that, if the Sultán would give orders, he would
proceed with a body of troops, and after reducing
him compel him to pay tribute." The Sultán replied to this, " that it was evident he, the Foujdár,
could never keep the country in proper order and
subjection," and he was accordingly dismissed from
his office, and Mahtab Khán, Bukhshi, was appointed in his place. The Sultán then returned to
his capital and took up his temporary residence in
the Durya Dowlut Baugh, or garden. The displaced Foujdár of Kalikote took up his quarters in
the Tukia, (the residence of religious men, probably from fear of his life) of Kadir Wuli, Pír Zada,
and after a short time resigned the loan of his life to
the Creator who gave it in the same place, and
agreeably to the orders of the Sultán was buried in
the Lal Baugh. Mahtab Khán Bukhshi, notwithstanding that he treated the inhabitants of that
country with great kindness, forwarded them assurances of safety and invited them to come to him ;
still the benighted heathens gave no credit to his

professions, and at the instigation of the people of
Koochi Bundur (Cochin) raised the head of rebellion in every quarter, and prepared themselves for
their defence.

The Sultán, also, no sooner became acquainted
with these circumstances than he marched with
his army by the route of Suttigal and Korical to
Kalikote, and appointed a detachment of his troops
to ravage the country of his enemies, and they accordingly lighted up the fire of oppression in all
the towns and villages in that neighbourhood. —
Verses, — " When they marched into that country,
they committed many cruel acts," they lighted up
such a fire of plunder, " that at once they burned
up every thing it contained." " From the hoofs of
their horses, the mountains and plains," — " were
all trodden to dust," " and even from the rocks,
trees, and stones," " deep sighs arose, and wailing."
After the whole country had been swept by the
besom of devastation, and when a host of the refractory and rebellious had been carried away by
the whirlwind of desolation, those who remained
being subdued, placed the ring * of servitude in the
ear of their lives, and with their hands tied together
submitted. During this time, a party of Kuzzaks
had spread themselves over the districts of Mali-

* See Deuteronomy, chap. xv. v. 17.

war and Trichinopoly, and had pillaged and burned
many towns of those districts. The collector of
revenue at Trichinopoly, therefore, addressed a
petition to the Sultán, stating that between the
government of the English company Buhadúr,
and that of the Khodádád, the foundations of peace,
and amity, were firmly established, — but, that at
the present time certain Kuzzaks, ignorant men,
had plundered the towns depending on that Souba
(Trichinopoly), and that it was their intention to
pluck up the root of the tree of friendship planted
in the hearts of the two governments, and that it
was indispensable they should be punished. In the
reply, the Sultán wrote him that *his* troops would
never plunder in any country without his orders,
and that it apparently must have been the Poligars
of the collector's own districts : — that they (the
Poligars) had been looking for an opportunity like
the present, and they had presumed, therefore, to
do the mischief ; that he, the Sultán, was occupied
in the regulation of his own territory, and the punishment of the refractory. In short, a month after
the subjection of the country had been effected,
the Sultán having acquired sufficient information
from his messengers and spies respecting the Port
of Cochin, he with the whole of his army marched
thither.

The people of Cochin being aware of the Sultan's
approach and intention, raised three or four batteries, (seemingly those of Cranganore and Aya-
kotta,) on the banks of the different rivers, and
surrounded them with deep ditches, and remained
ready for battle, occupying the road with a very
strong body of archers and musketeers ; — at
nightfall of the day [b] on which he arrived (apparently), the Sultán ordered his troops to assault
and take the batteries, and they, with honourable
emulation and the greatest bravery, took them,
and the Sultán immediately moved on to a place
where two rivers crossed the road, and where
the enemy had built a wall across the road of
the ford, and had stationed themselves to defend it. The passage of the tide also above and
where the water of the sea flowed into the river,
was blocked up by a mound, so that the water
was stopped in its passage, and the bed. of the
river became dry. But, although several of the
Sultan's confidential servants, such as Turbeut
Alí Khán, and others, took the liberty to represent
that in front the road was bad and intersected by
the beds of deep rivers, and that a night expedition was not safe, and God forbid that the enemy
should gain an advantage and the Ghazies be de-

[b] December 28, 1789.

feated ; still their advice was disregarded and the representation of no one met with approval, and the Sultán getting into his Pálkí with two Risalas, and two thousand regular horse, proceeded onwards forthwith, dark as it was. The Sultán's faithful soldiers now at one assault with their swords and muskets, drove the enemy before them and by the help of ropes and ladders, scaled and took the first works, and as the enemy lost the power of resistance and fled before the Mussulmans, towards the fort, the Sultán halted where he was, and ordered his Hurkuras (messengers) to bring up the Kushoons and artillery. As soon as these arrived, two Kushoons forming the advanced guard, being in all points prepared for action, were ordered on, and the remainder of the Kushoons kept in reserve; — when at about daybreak all of a sudden the treacherous enemy finding this the critical moment for them to obtain the victory, cut down the mound, which (as before mentioned) they had raised above in order to stop out the sea, and the tide rushing in with great violence filled up the rivers to the brim, and the road of succour and assistance to the advanced division of the Sultán's troops was cut off.

In this time the enemy attacked the Sultán's troops on all sides with arrows and musketry, and caused incalculable distress and confusion among them, and, however vigorously they strove to repel their infidel assailants it was of no avail, and they were overwhelmed with all kinds of evil and calamity, but notwithstanding all this, three or four hundred brave horsemen, men of good families, gave substantial proofs of their valour, and were all killed and wounded in front of the Sultán. At this time Kumruddín Khán, who was present with the Sultán, by adjurations and entreaties falling at his feet, took him out of his Pálkí, and by the strong exertion of loyalty and fidelity, caused him to be carried through the water to the opposite side of the river, and then constrained him to turn his steps towards his camp. But of those present in that battle not one man ever returned safe to the presence. The Sultán's Pálkí with its bed, the great seal of the exchequer and a dagger were taken by the infidels.

Some report that the Sultán's turban was in the Pálkí, but it is a great mistake, for the Sultán's turban at that time was upon his fortunate [c] head, and the coloured turban which fell into the hands of the enemy belonged to one of his footmen, who ran before the Pálkí, and who was accidentally killed by an arrow, or a musket ball, and his tur-

كرامت پيكر [c]

ban falling near the Pálkí, the benighted infidels thought it was the Sultán's, and placed it in the Pálkí: — In short the Sultán and Kumruddín Khán escaped out of the whirlpool of their fortunes, and the rest of the Kháns, such as Turbeut Alí Khán, Muhammad Omr, Urzbegi, and, Sayeed Khán the Durogha of the treasury, &c. were never after heard of.

The Sultán's anger at this untoward event was excessive, but having caused his drums to beat for victory (as if he had gained one) he directed bridges of wood, cut down from the Jungle to be made, and having by their means crossed the rivers, he brought upon his enemies a resemblance to the days of judgment small and great.

The Sipahdárs and Mowkubdárs, now, according to their orders, attacked the enemy from different points to the extent or along a front of three miles, and with their keen swords, relieved the shoulders of all the infidels they met (man or boy) from the weight of their heads.[d]

As the power of resistance had now quitted the heathens, they, fearing the might and greatness of the Sultán and his army, fled to Maliwar, abandoning both their country and wealth. The victorious Sultán, therefore, now entered the walls of the

[d] Meaning they gave no quarter.

port of Cochin, and took possession of every particle of the property remaining therein, as the
arms, stores, guns, &c. A nutmeg tree also, which
was growing in the fort, he took up with the roots,
and having wrapped it in rice straw, despatched
it with the greatest care to Seringaputtun, and it
was there planted in the Lal Bagh, or garden ; —
it did not, however, thrive, but soon died.

CHAPTER XIII.

An account of the advance of an army under the command of
General Meadows to the aid of the Raja of Maliwar, and the
battles fought between the English army and that of the Sultán ; —
the death of Boorhanuddín Sipahsalar, who was slain near the
Fort of Sutti Mungul, the march of the Royal Standard towards
the Payanghaut, and an account of the different victories gained
about that time, 1205, Hijri. — A. D. 1790.

WHEN the conquering Sultán had completed the
conquest of this country (Cochin, or Travancore,)
he demanded tribute from the Poligar of Maliwar,
and despatched a body of Kuzzaks to plunder and
take possession of that woody country. The Poligar, therefore, trembling like a reed from fear of
the Sultán's sharp sword, now sought aid and redress from the Governor of Madras and General
Meadows was appointed to oppose the Sultán,
the destroyer of his enemies, and advanced to
Nuthur Nuggur (Trichinopoly).

From that place, however, with the aid of the
Poligar of Maliwar, who had assembled his army
and was ready for action, he next marched forward by the route of Karoor to attack the Sultán.

Accordingly, in the vicinity of Koimbetore and
Sutti Mungal, he fell in with the advanced guard
of the conquering army, and a sharp action followed, and from the clangour of the drums and
trumpets, and the roar of the discharges of musketry,
rockets, and cannon, the clamour of the day of
resurrection arose from both armies, and the Kuzzaks having surrounded the followers of the British
army in the forest of Dindigul, after killing and
wounding many, took prisoners some of the soldiers with their women, muskets, and baggage, the
latter tied in bundles on their heads.   Among these
were some Muhammadan women, who from want
of shame and the fear of an hereafter, had gone
aside from their religion, and had given up their
impure bodies to the lust of men of other religions,
(this refers to Europeans, I believe,) and they according to the orders of the Sultán were impaled.
On this day, however, the troops of both armies
after repelling the charges made by each other
remained on equal terms, and in the evening the
General taking up ground at the foot of the mountains encamped there.

   The army of the Sultan, however, surrounded
the General's troops closely, and harassed them
continually, by driving in their foraging parties,
and stopping their supplies.   The next day, the

General marched on and took the small fort of
Sutti Mungul (from which the Sultán had previously withdrawn the garrison), and left two
battalions there under the command of Major
(Chalmers, or) Chambers. He halted at this place
a short time, and then marched towards Koimbetore,
at which place at that time the Sultán himself was
encamped ; — at hearing this news the Sultán, at
the presumption of the general, was much excited,
and with the whole of his army marched to meet
him, and having taken up his ground for a regular field engagement, remained ready for action.
On that day, however, the general did not advance,
but encamped on the banks of the river Bho-
wani ; * during this a body of English troops, which
had been assembled at Seoram at first under the
command of Colonel Kelly, lost its commanding
officer, who died, and Colonel Maxwell, who had
lately arrived from Bengal with five battalions of
Native infantry, and a thousand Europeans, was
appointed to command in his place, and with the
subsidiary troops of the Poligars, that is the Poligars of Kalistri, Vinkutgiri, &c. advanced by the
route of Rai Vellore, and Amboor Gurh, towards
Koimbetore, and on the route leaving small garrisons in Wanumbari and Tripatore, marched to

* One copy says, the Sultán did not advance.

the Ghaut, or pass of Tuppoor. The Sultán on being made acquainted with this movement, detached Syud Sáhib, Sipahsalar, to arrest the progress of that body of troops, and he himself followed with the same intention, and marched in the direction of Dhurumpoori. The aforesaid Sipahsalar, however, had no sooner made a forced march with his division, than the Colonel (Maxwell), who was marching on the road to Dhurumpoori, suddenly countermarched and retired towards Gugungurh. Syud Ghuffar, therefore, with his Kuzzaks preceding the army moved on, and near that place fell in with and attacked the advanced guard of the English force, and cut them off, taking prisoners one hundred and fifty troopers and two hundred infantry.

The Colonel, therefore, on that day, kept the woody and hilly ground, and on the next marched towards Kauveri Puttun ; when, however, he saw the Sultán's troops surrounding him on all sides, he kept close to the hilly country and marched in the direction of the Ghaut of Tippoor, and General Meadows proceeding by forced marches to join him, the two officers met at the foot of the Ghaut near Kaveripoor. At the period, however, of the junction of these officers, the faithful servants of the Sultán brought up their Kushoons between them, and displaying great bravery, obtained many advantages. The English officers also with their troops charged the victorious army and fought desperately until the Sultán himself, with his Assud Illáhi Kushoons, (or brigades) and artillery, vigorously attacked their rear and reduced them to such straights as left them no means or mode of escape.

The General, therefore, formed his army into a square, and taking his cattle and followers into the centre, marched by the route of Marpaich again towards Suttimungul : — in short, after the space of two or three months, in which the two armies had been continually doing all they could to distress and destroy each other ; the supplies and provisions of the English army were exhausted, and the days of scarcity shewed their faces, — the hope of further convoys of provisions or stores from any quarter now having vanished, the general with all his troops marched towards Trichinopoly. The victorious army, however, stopped his progress in the plain of Suttimungul, and so surrounded and so vigorously attacked him, that most of the officers (apparently the English), the lovers of justice and candour, expressed their astonishment at their valour. The keen sword and musket of the brave Mussulmans destroyed many of the infidels, and it went very near that a total defeat and dispersion had fallen upon that army, when night came on and the veil of darkness fell before the faces of the fearless combatants, and both armies drew back their hands from the fight, and the General conceiving that day's march had been as difficult as if it had been on the tail of a serpent (alluding seemingly to the name of the road Mar-paich, but there is some difference in the MSS. here,) halted where he was for the night.

When the Turk, or king of day, (the sun) marched with his army of light from the plains of the east towards the west, (in allusion apparently to the original country of the Turks,) the General marched forward, — he, however, left all his heavy baggage on the ground, and the Kuzzak horse and the Kushoons again were put in motion, and they sur-rounded him, and commenced the action like true and faithful soldiers; when, as fate decreed, Boorhan-uddín the Sipahsalar, who commanded the advanced guard of the victorious army, proceeded in front of the whole on horseback to examine the face of the field of battle, and to find ground qualified, or con-venient for a cavalry charge. It happened, that in front of him was a dry bed of a river, in which some English soldiers were stationed in ambush, and these seeing horsemen near them, fired a volley at them, and a ball from one of their unlucky muskets entered

his valiant forehead, and he died, and his soul sped
to its eternal abode.   The troops with him now retired, and laying his body in a pálkí, and proceeding to the presence, reported the circumstances of
his death.   The Sultán, who had a tender heart, at
the death of that strong arm of his prosperity, was
much grieved; nay, so afflicted, that he shed many
tears, and, therefore, on that day he restrained his
troops from fighting any more, and however much
the Sipahdárs and other officers desired that they
might receive orders to attack and charge, and by
that means decide the fortune of the day, still, no
orders came, and they rubbed the hands of grief
one upon the other.   In this time the General
(Meadows) perceiving that his enemies were timid
and slow, marched on without delay, and entered
the Fort of Trichinopoly.   The Sultán now consigned the troops of Boorhanuddín Khán to
Kumruddín Khán, and detached him to take the
Fort of Suttimungul, while he himself turned the
direction of his standards towards the Payanghaut
and encamped in the neighbourhood of Turwur
Paleh, and from thence detached his cavalry to
plunder and destroy the towns (dependencies) of
Trichinopoly and those of Tanjore.   The Gene-
tal now halted where he was for sometime, and
then by the route of the sea-shore retired with

his troops to Madras. The Sultán, the destroyer of his enemies, now followed this army and arrived at Jingee and Purmokul Gurh. In the mean time Kumruddín Khán, as soon as he had taken leave of the Sultán, immediately commenced the siege of the little fort of Suttimungul, attacking it on all sides (it should be Koimbetore, according to Colonel Marriott) and after battering and destroying the walls prepared for the assault. Before, however, the victorious troops could take the fort by that mode of attack, the officer in command there, who was much distressed for want of ammunition, provisions, and water, despatched a messenger to the Khán, and made terms of peace, and after the sanction of agreements and covenants the fort was delivered up to the agents of the Sultán, and the Khán, having made over the fort to the charge of the Asof of Sulaumubád, himself with his prisoners, returned to the presence. In result, orders were issued that the officers with Major Chalmers should be placed in confinement, and sent to Seringaputtun, and that his Sipahees should be incorporated in the Sultán's Kushoons, and this was accordingly done.

As soon as the General had arrived at Madras, the Sultán detached several large bodies of troops from his army to plunder and take possession of

different parts of the country, and accordingly
Kumruddín Khán was sent to take the Hill Fort
of Purmokul Gurh, the walls of which had formerly
been battered down, but had lately been replaced
by fortifications of earth, and an officer who had in
former time been taken prisoner by the late Nawáb
with two hundred men, was appointed to command
there. Kumruddín, therefore, according to orders
with his own division of troops marched thither,
and thousands of the poor inhabitants and peasantry of the neighbourhood, relying in the strength
of the English garrison, having sought refuge on
the hill were plundered and destroyed. The cause
was this, that immediately on the arrival of the
Sultán's troops, the officer commanding in the fort
frightened at their great numbers, and recollecting
his former perils and hardships, under pretence of
a violent headache, took to his chamber and left
the defence of the fort to the Soubadárs and other
officers, and they seeing from the want of order
and arrangement in the store and provision departments, that there was no chance of successfully
defending the fort, agreeably to the wishes of their
officer, peaceably surrendered it. The whole of
the people, therefore, who had sought refuge there
were placed in confinement, and at that time Kishen
Rao, the Mutsuddi, or clerk of the Sultán's trea-

sury, arriving, he exacted the sum of ten thousand rupees from these poor people, and then released them. The officer and garrison of Purmokul, were also allowed to proceed to Madras.

172

CHAPTER XIV.

An account of the arrival from Bengal of the Governor-General, Earl Cornwallis, Bahadúr, — the Commander-in-Chief of the
English army, and his confederacy with Nizám Alí Khán, and
the Mahrattas. Also, the march of the confederates to attack on
all sides, and root up the power of the Khodádád (the Kingdom
of Mysore,) and the conquest of the Forts and Towns of the Balaghaut. Also, the Battles fought between the army of the Sultán
and those of the confederates with other events of the year, 1206,
Hijri. — A. D. 1791.

THE maritime intelligence department of the
English government now reported to the Commander-in-Chief of their army, the march of the
Sultán to the country of the Karnatic Payanghaut, that the whole of the province had been
swept by the tempest of desolation ; — that the
troops of the victorious army had occupied it on
all sides, and that General Meadows, after some
exertions, from the want of provisions and other
stores, being without resource, had returned to
Madras ; — that if the enemy were not soon ex-
pelled, there was great danger of a general rebellion in that country, and that it would then quickly
pass out of the hands of the English government.

About this time, also, Aboo Kasim Khán, called also Mír i Alum, the embassador of Nizám Alí Khán, who had been sent to Bengal previously, by the policy of Mushír ul Moolk,ꞌ the prime Minister of the chief of Hydurabád, to stimulate and incite the Commander-in-chief of the English army to the destruction of the Khodádád state, finding every thing favourable to his views, exerted himself to the utmost, and the Commander-in-chief, or rather the Governor-general wrote to the Nizám of Hy-durabád, and the Chief of Poona (the Paishwa) recommending their conquering, and then dividing amongst them, the whole of the Balaghaut pro-vinces, and then despatched orders to prepare military equipment, and collect troops to the Governor, &c. of Madras ; — he himself making preparations at the same time.

The Nizám and Mahrattas who were looking out for an invitation to seize and plunder the wealth and territory of those who had no friends to assist them, in conformity to the suggestion of the Governor-general, with one accord assembled their troops and made all necessary preparations for war. The En-glish officers too, in collecting their stores and muni-tions of war, each being separately appointed to his work, made all things ready with great labour, and

عالم خراب ꞌ

Colonel Read, the Darogha of the intelligence
department, who was appointed to the command
of Amboor Gurh, with great address, and by the
liberal distribution of money, sweet words, and
kind actions, brought over to his side the whole of
the Poligars of the Balaghaut, who from the oppression and cruelty of the late Nawáb, and the tyrannical character of the Sultán had abandoned their
own country, and had sought refuge in the towns
of the Karnatic Payanghaut; such as the Poligar
of Gungoondi Pala; the sons of Bhyreh Koor, the
Poligar of Chuk Balapoor, Pud Naír, the Poligar
of Vinkut Giri Kote, who was residing at Charkul;
Shunk Rayel, or Rawul, the Chief of Punganoor,
and besides these, the Poligars of Khut Koomnír,
Mudun Pulli, Ánikul, Oonkus Giri, Cheel Náík,
&c. all being dispossessed of their lands, received
written assurances of protection, and were despatched to their own districts on condition they
should collect and forward supplies of forage and
provisions to the English army; and they also
received authority to retake or recover (by any
means) their own districts and Talookas : — and,
notwithstanding the severe restrictions in the Balaghaut, where without passes from the heads of districts, a man was not permitted to go from one
town to another, he Colonel Read, obtained maps

of the whole of the country, by sending clever spies
and able moonshis at great expense, dressed as
merchants into that country, and by their agency
or mediation, also, several chiefs and officers of
the Sirkar Khodádád, having been brought over to
his interest, he sat waiting the arrival of the Governor-general, and although a certain Syud Imám,
previously private intelligencer to Colonel Read,
who was residing at the capital (Puttun) had obtained employment in the Sultan's service; still,
he wrote and despatched correct intelligence on all
subjects, continually to Colonel Read, and he also
had assembled a number of traitors to his aid;
when all at once the dish of his detection and
shame appeared from beneath the blanket, (in allusion to some Persian custom, or game, apparently,)
for his treachery by reason of some correction he
had given to a boy, his servant, or slave, was pub-
lished to the world ; and at length certain of the
Sultán's faithful servants seized him and his boy,
and brought them before the presence, and detailed
all the circumstances of his treachery ; this doomed
man, therefore, fell under the heavy displeasure
of the Sultán, and he was asked by him, what have
you been doing ? — " If you tell the truth you
may by that means save your life for a time." In
these difficulties this foolish man made up a story

with truth and falsehood intermixed, and wrote
the names of several officers who had leagued with
him in his treachery, and presented them to the
Sultán, and according to this list of names, fifteen
persons, such as Lall Khán Bukhshi of Punganore;
Mír Nuzzur Alí, Mokubdár, and his brother, and
Ismael Khán Risaldár, &c. were seized and given
over in charge to the executioner, and after the
proof or establishment of the secret intelligence
writer's guilt (Islám Khán's) the Sultán asked him,
" how he who had eaten his salt could have acted
so treacherously, and what punishment he thought
such conduct deserved ?" The culprit, however,
returned no answer, and the Sultán then said, " send
this gentleman ⁵ with the rest of his companions ;"
and he was also put to death.

Another person also, named Imám Uddín, a
news writer, who had been employed in the same
work and who resided at Kolar and Nundi Gurh,
hearing this news at night, fled from that place to
Kurumpaut, depending on Sautgurh. Still, however, notwithstanding the disclosure of all this
treachery, and the execution of his hired dependants, Colonel Read did not abstain from his in-
trigues and projects. As soon as intelligence, that
the troops, provisions, and stores were all ready,

⁵ بزرگ زادہ

reached the Governor-General, he immediately
with five thousand Bengal Sipahees, and two thousand Europeans, embarked on board ship and sailed
to Madras, and after remaining there a month, he
marched, accompanied by twenty-four regiments
of Native Infantry; six thousand Europeans, and
three thousand regular cavalry, and with great discipline and order, arrived at Rai Vellore, en route
to the conquest of the Balaghaut.

In the meantime, the Sultán while he remained
encamped near Turwadi, had entered into some
negotiation with the French of Pondicherri for aid
and support when his spies brought him intelligi-
gence of the march of the Governor-General.
In consequence, therefore, of this report, Muhammad Khán Bukhshi was detached with a large body
of troops, and marched by the route of the Chun-
guma Ghaut to Tripatoor, — the fort of which was
garrisoned by one hundred English Sipahees, commanded by an European officer, and three hundred
foot, belonging to the Poligar of Kalistri, under
the command of Ankupa Naír. This fort, therefore, Muhammad Khán closely surrounded, and
thus endeavoured to block up the road of escape
to the garrison. The officer in the fort and the
Naír, however, after counting the stars all night,
before sunrise next morning, evacuated the fort

N

and took the road to Amboor Gurh. Muhammad Khán's horse, however followed them close,
and fell in with them near the foot of the hills of
Jowadi Pala, and at one charge defeated them.
The officer and the Naír were taken prisoners,
and the horse returned. At this time, Nizám Alí
Khán, with forty thousand horse and twenty thousand foot, accompanied by his most trusty Amírs,
and his sons Alijah, and Sekundur Jah, marched
from Hydurabád and encamped at Pankul, and he
thence despatched his Amírs with a large force in
advance to conquer the possessions of the Sultán.
The Commander-in-chief of the English army had
effected the passage of his army by the Ghaut, or
pass of Moglievinkut Giri, and had posted detachments in the towns of Morewakul,[h] Kolar and
Huskote, and marching on had arrived at Kishen
Rajpoor, which is three kose from Bangalore; —
when the Sultán receiving intelligence of his progress, made a forced march to stop him.

It is not to be omitted here, that when the
French heard of the movements of the English
army, and the plunder and ravage of the Payanghaut; from their extreme regard and friendship
for the Sultán, they were very unwilling that any
injury should be sustained by his army; — they,

[h] Called by Colonel Marriott, Malwaggle.

therefore, determined to send him a thousand men
of their nation to assist him, that in all his measures
they might be ready to serve under his orders ; —
some, however, of the Sultán's servants, upon whose
advice he placed the greatest reliance, with the
view of manifesting their loyalty, represented that
the throne and crown of that sun of the constellation of kingly power and greatness, (*i. e.* the
Sultán) would rise and culminate without the countenance or assistance of others, and that the conquering Sultán did not in any way require the aid
of French troops :[1] —·that, moreover, it was proper to consider to whom these troops had ever
been faithful, and what prince with their assistance
had been supported and established ? — By these
specious arguments, they so effectually influenced
the Sultán, that he rejected the offer of assistance
from the French, and with his own troops only,
marched to repel his powerful enemies, and the
same night detached his Kuzzaks and rocketeers to
surround and fire into the camp of the English
army, while he himself proceeded to Bangalore.
The Kuzzaks, therefore, remained all night attacking, or sniping and throwing rockets into the English camp, until the morning when the English

[1] It appears clear the author thinks he had better have accepted them.

Commander-in-chief, (Lord Cornwallis), without
taking much notice of them, marched on and left
a place full of fear and danger, and that day
encamped at Hussoor, and the next day again
marched to the north eastward, and encamped at
the distance of one fursung from the town of Bangalore.

The Sultán now, therefore, appointed Syud
Humíd Sipahdár with his Kushoon to the charge
of the second or lower fort, and Muhammad Khán
Bukhshi before mentioned, and a certain Buhadúr
Khán, who had previously been Foujdár of Kishingiri was appointed governor of the upper fort
or citadel, and Shaikh Oonsur was sent with him.

The Sultán then marched on to the vicinity
of Tunkri, where he determined to encamp, and
directed his victorious standards to be planted
there; — neither the Sultán's tents nor those of
any others, however, were yet pitched, most of the
horse were scattered in search of forage, and only
three or four Kushoons of the Jysh and Ussud Illahi
infantry, and two or three thousand stable horse
(household troops) remained with the Sultán, when
Colonel Floy (Floyd) with the whole of the English
regular cavalry advanced and charged into the Sultán's camp, and all at once arrived in front of the
Tope Khána or park of artillery. The artillery

and the officers of the Kushoons, however, now immediately formed up and arrested their progress, and with their guns and muskets soon quelled their pride and insolence, and compelled them to retreat quickly.

It happened also that the colonel abovementioned was struck with a musket ball in the throat and the wound depriving him of the power of speech,[k] the other officers commanding regiments, not being able to continue the engagement, turned their faces from the field of battle. The brave horse now pursued and attacked them, with the greatest vigour with sword and spear, and four hundred English troopers with their horses were taken prisoners; — the remainder spared by the sword, fled, rising and falling to the main body of the army. The next day Colonel Moorhouse[1] and General Meadows with a strong body of troops attacked the town (the Pettah of Bangalore) and after the sacrifice of thousands of men on both sides, and after an attack of six hours, the town was with great gallantry taken, and so large a quantity of spoil, such as gold, jewels, &c. fell into the hands of the captors, that penury and want were thenceforward discharged or struck off

[k] See Colonel Welsh's Journal or Reminiscences.—Vol. I, p. 9.

[1] مورس

from the muster roll of the English army. The
colonel before mentioned (Moorhouse) was killed
by wounds from musket balls during the storm.
After this, the English collected the materials for
their operations such as fascines, stockades, &c.
round the town and commenced raising batteries,
and for fourteen days they battered the fort continually.

During this time, however, Kumr uddín Khán,
agreeably to the Sultán's orders, with his own
division of troops, remained in the vicinity of
Busoon Gori to render all the assistance he could
to the besieged. When, however, the walls of the
fort were battered down, the Sultán became very
anxious and fearful for the result, and therefore
gave orders that the fort should be evacuated;
Kishn Rao accordingly was sent there and he
brought away all the property of the state, such
as the guns, the money, &c. with the store and
other departments; and they were despatched to
Seringaputtun, leaving only one Kushoon and two
thousand irregular troops, (Ahshám) with their artillery in the fort. It was, therefore, determined
by the advice of certain of the Sultán's counsellors,
that the defence of the fort, should be left to Monsieur Lally, and that Kumr uddín Khán and Syud
Sáhib with a strong force should be appointed to

make a demonstration against the English army,
while the Sultán himself should march to arrest
the progress of the Moghuls (the Nizám's troops)
and the Mahrattas. In pursuance of this arrangement the French officer (Lally) actually marched,
and had arrived at the tank or reservoir[m] of the
canal, when Kishn Rao, and some other traitors
becoming acquainted with this plan gave a hint
to the English Hurkaras, who were always about
them habited as their own servants, and they immediately apprised the guards in the trenches that
now the time had arrived to make an assault and
take the fort. Kishn Rao after this left the fort,
and at the bank of the tank above mentioned,
meeting Monsieur Lally, took him by the hand
and kept him in conversation about trifles, while
the officers in the trenches as soon as they received
the information before mentioned, immediately got
their troops in readiness and a little after midnight,
all at once made their attack. Syud Humíd the
Sipahdár and the Killadárs (commanders of the
garrison) according to the directions of the traitor
Kishn Rao, had allowed their men who were all
prepared to defend the fort, to go to their quarters
and cook their victuals, and, therefore, except a
few sentinels, no one remained at their posts, but

كاريز [m]

notwithstanding their helpless condition they boldly
advanced to repel their assailants, and drove them
back from the chain of the gate. The Europeans,
however, having been quickly supplied with the
wine, (or rather spirituous liquor), which inspires
courage, returned to the charge, and by the time
the brave garrison had assembled, they had stormed
and mounted the walls and towers. The Syud
being without his men and seeing he could not
maintain his ground, escaped and joined the army.
The two Killadárs with forty or fifty of their men
planting their feet manfully at the gate, were there
slain, as was Shaíkh Boodhun Risaladár, after giving
manifold proofs of his courage and fidelity. Shaíkh
Oonsur Sipahdár and the Naíkwars (the Naírs or
Hindu chiefs) and soldiers of the fort were taken
prisoners. The fort, therefore, was captured and
the garrison with their women and children, and
their money and property of all kinds fell into the
possession of the English soldiers, and the women
were given up to violation.[n]   Although at the time
of the assault the Sultán mounted his horse, and
with his troops stood ready to engage the enemy;
still, he restrained his hand from shedding the blood
of God's people, and although the Khán above-
mentioned (Kumruddín) and Syud Sáhib often re-

ناموسها تاراج دادنله "

quested orders to charge the English troops, the
Sultán replied that the time would come by and
by, for that the favorable opportunity had passed,
and that they were on no account to allow their
men to fall into disorder. The next morning the
Sultán marched on, and placing the jungul or
forest of Makri in his rear, encamped there. In
short, after three or four days, the Commander-in-
Chief of the English army appointed a garrison of
two or three thousand native infantry and six
hundred Europeans to the charge of the fort, and
leaving there part of the stores of his army, marched
by the route of Yuloonka to cover and take into
his possession the supplies of provisions and cattle,
which the Poligars of the north, such as the chiefs
of Chuk Balapoor, Punganoor, Khut Komnere and
Muddun Pulli had collected according to their engagements, and who with great gallantry had dispossessed the Sultán's officers some by fair, and
some by foul means of the forts, towns and villages,
which had been previously their hereditary possessions, and were now enjoying themselves in their
success without fear or restraint. Although in the
neighbourhood of the place above mentioned, Kumr
uddín Khán with a large force had possession, or
command of the roads, and laboured hard to ob-
struct and defeat the English, and that the Kuz-

zaks also constantly hung on the rear of their
army, and put to confusion and dispersed their
followers, and cattle, plundering them of property
to a great amount, and also, that the troops in
general, in repelling their enemies used every exertion;—still, the days of conquest did not come
to the Sultán's aid, but hid themselves from his sight.

The Commander-in-Chief of the English army
that day halted on the same ground; the next day
he moved on to the neighbourhood of Yousufabad,
otherwise called Dewun Hulli, where he encamped,
and having despatched an officer with a party of
men to the fort, and having brought over the
officer commanding there to surrender without resistance, he took possession of the fort, and divided
the stores of grain and other articles among his
own men. After the lapse of two days the Commander-in-Chief again marched and encamped
near Balapoor Khoord, but the officer in charge of
the fort there, agreeably to the Sultán's orders
evacuated the fort before the arrival of the English
army and with all the infantry, Náíkwars, and
stores, retired to the Hill Fort of Nundi and consequently the advanced guard of the English took
possession of the fort without opposition, and the
stores and provisions that were lying about fell
into their hands. The Commander-in-Chief here

taking pity on the misfortunes of Ram Swamy
Koor, to whom the possession of that district belonged in hereditary right, made it over to him
with the fort, and its dependencies, on condition
that he paid yearly a tribute of one lakh of rupees.
He then marched on towards Ambajee Droog and
as after a very long time his (Ram Swamy's) good
fortune had favoured him and the capital of his
district fell into his hands, at a fortunate moment
he entered the fort, and after repairing and making
arrangements for its security, he left there six hundred foot under his own followers and strengthen-
ing it with stores and artillery proceeded to Tulkai
Goonda, a town or fort seated in the midst of a
dense jungle. The conquering Sultán now ordered
Ancupa Naír and the English officers, who had
been taken prisoners at the fort of Tripatoor, to
be delivered over to the executioners, and Jogi
Pundit the nephew of Achna Pundit the Náíb of
the Souba of Arkat, who during the reign of the
Sultán, had been advanced to high dignity and had
received the title of Raja Ramchundur, and was
also appointed Serishtadár of the whole of the
Talookas of Bangalore, but who from his evil destiny, had not acted in conformity to the orders of
the Sultán, but had leagued with the enemy, was
put to death in company with the Poligars of

Hurpun Hully, and Rai Droog, who had been imprisoned, and were executed because for some days the fire of the Sultán's wrath burned fiercely, at the bare mention of the names of the Poligars. Kishn Rao was at this time sent to take charge of the capital (Seringaputtun), and to despatch money for the payment of the troops, while the Sultán himself with the army and its departments marched in pursuit of the English army to Bala-poor Khoord. The splendour of the Sultán's standard, however, no sooner shone on that fort, than the garrison with great folly beat to arms and sounded their trumpets on the ramparts, at the same time howling and barking like a pack of hounds. The Sultán, therefore, determined to punish them, and ordered his brave troops to the assault, and they with ladders and ropes soon esca-laded the walls and conquered their enemies, for although the garrison with one heart and hand giving up all care for their lives, fought so despe-rately that two thousand Ghazies bit the dust, they were at length subdued, and gave their heads and breasts as an oblation to the sword and spear, and three hundred foot soldiers who were taken alive, according to the orders of the Sultán for an example to others, had their hands and feet cut off, or broken with saws and hatchets by his exe-

cutioners and they were then left on the ground.
In a moment, therefore, the clamour of the day of
judgement arose from these unfortunate men, and
after this (most unjust and cruel act) the Sultán
marched from that place and encamped in the
neighbourhood of Sulket.

The Commander-in-Chief of the English army,
Lord Cornwallis, in the mean time had taken the
fort of Ambajee Droog from the Killadár Muhammad Khán Boorka, and had razed the works to
the ground, and after that encamped there two or
three days. The Poligars who have been before
mentioned in this period, forwarded provisions and
cattle to the English camp, and received great
praise and reward for their service. The Sipahsalar or Commander-in-Chief of the English, then
marched on and encamped near the fort of Murg
Mulla, when Assud Alí Khán and Bhar Mul, the
Dewán of Mushír ul Moolk, with five thousand
horse, entered the English camp, and the next day
they marched from that place by the road of Chin-
tumani and Morwakul to Vinkut Giri Pala. The
brave and powerful Sultán with his victorious
army had at this time turned the head of his
generous steed towards the English army with the
intention to attack it, when a jasoos, or spy dressed
in a suit of mourning arrived, sent by his mother

from Seringaputtun, and this man in private informed the Sultán that the villain Kishn Rao con-
spiring with some other traitors, had so concerted
and arranged that probably by this time a sedition
had broken out in the capital, or would soon break
out, the repression of which it would not be very
easy to accomplish,—he having followed the path
of the rejected° Khundi Rao, and had sent for a
large body of English troops from Bombay, and
that the Queen, (the Sultán's wife), had given up
all hope or care of her life,—at hearing this intelligence the Sultán despatched Syud Sáhib with
a body of troops to provide for the security and
order of his capital.

° مردود

CHAPTER XV.

An account of the reduction to order and obedience of the Capital, and the merited punishment of the Traitor Kishn Rao, with the arrival of the Sultán there. — Also, the Invasion and ravage of the Mussulman Territory (Mysore) by the Moghuls and Mahrattas, with other events of the same year 1206, Hijri. — A. D. 1791.

WHEN Syud Sáhib received orders to depart, he proceeded forthwith by the route of the Makri Jungul and Rai Droog, and arrived at the capital of the Sultán, Seringaputtun, at mid-night, and placed his encampment on this side the river, while he himself with a few friends, and four or five hundred horse advanced to the gate of the fort, and before the appearance of the first light of the morning, called out to the guard at the gate to open it. As it happened, that Assud Khán Risaldár and other loyal subjects of the Sultán had been appointed to the charge of this gate, they pleased at the arrival of the Syud, opened the wickets, and he entered, and having stationed parties of his horse over different departments of the state, he proceeded to pay his respects to the Sultán's mother, and she seated

herself in the Hall of audience. At this time the
commander of the troops at the capital, who was
deeply implicated in the treason of the Brahman,
finding his secret disclosed to the world, immediately repaired to the Syud, and boasting of his
own fidelity and loyalty, and condemning the folly
and treason of the Brahman, persisted in demanding
that he should be imprisoned. The Syud, therefore,
despatched a Chobedár[p] to summon Kishn Rao, to
the Hall of audience or Durbar, and, as he, being
aware of his danger, returned for answer, that it was
unusual and unreasonable the Syud should send him
orders, that he had nothing to do with him : — his
answer confirming the suspicion before entertained
of his treachery, the Syud ordered the persons present to proceed to his house and seize him, and
they forcing their way into his house and breaking
open the door of his apartment, which he had
bolted, or secured in the inside, they with their
swords and muskets put him to death, and threw
his body into the drain of the bazaar, and his house
was plundered, and the property found in it carried
to the treasury. During the last moments, however, of this fiend, he said, — " I have lighted up a
fire, which as long as the Sultán lives will not be

---

[p] A man who carries a silver or gold-headed stick before chiefs
in India and is employed as a messenger.

extinguished :" — this, alas, was but too true. His wife who was beautiful, faithful, and virtuous, of her own accord, despatched a message to the Queen, (زمانه ملكه) and sought refuge with her, and by the mediation of that veiled lady of the curtain of chastity, and honour, she was placed in the Haram Serai of the Sultán. Another person has, however, told this story in a different way ; — he states that when the villain Brahman, notwithstanding the favours and honours showered on him, was seeking the ruin of the Sultán ; his virtuous wife becoming acquainted with his designs, and being disgusted at the base ingratitude and treachery of her husband, despatched a verbal message by her nurse to the Sultán's mother, informing her of his absurd and foolish machinations : — and some, who say that the Sultán after the slaying of the traitor Brahman, tyrannically forced his wife to enter his Seraglio, make a false charge, and lying accusation, for at the time of the death of her husband, if she had not been willing to go to the Sultán, would she not under some pretence, or by some contrivance have put herself to death ; [9] — but omitting this, could she not have made away with herself when sent for to the Haram.

But to return, — the Sultán after the departure

---

[9] The author supposes this mode of reasoning perfectly conclusive.

of Syud Sáhib, appointed Kumr uddín Khán to command a body of ten thousand horse, that he should take every opportunity to attack and harass the army and baggage of the strangers, while he himself marched towards his capital to restore order there. The General in Chief of the English in the course of three days, despatched all his Bunjaras and Lemauns,' and his hired cattle to Amboor Gurh, and sending for all articles of necessity, such as stores of grain, bread, artillery, and ammunition, he marched by the route of Beed Mungul, and Maloor, to Bangalore. The Sultán's Commander-in-chief. marching towards the English army, gave orders to his Kuzzaks to disguise themselves so as to appear like the troops of the Nizám, and attack the rear guard of the enemy, which was composed of the Moghul or Nizám's horse, and two regiments of English cavalry, and they like hungry lions among sleeping deer, fell on them and entirely defeated them, taking five thousand bullocks laden with grain, and two hundred Moghul horse. In short, every day the Sillahdárs, Kuzzaks, Afghans, and Dukkanees, threw themselves like as the moth throws himself on the candle, on the pickets, and advanced parties of the

' Men who carry grain about for sale, on bullocks, the latter term, however, is not, I believe, used for Bunjaras in Hindostan.'

two armies (the English and Moghul), and multitudes of men became the food of the unsparing
sword, spear and musket, and the route of communication, and the passage of supplies to the
enemy were completely shut and blocked up, so
indeed that night or day, no one could quit their
camp, — and as during the course of this contention and warfare, by God's assistance, from the
exceeding bravery of the soldiers of the victorious
army, great fear fell on the minds of the enemy,
the pride and insolence in which they had indulged, because the Sultán did not oppose them in
person, was now changed to fear and trembling,
and they became timid, doubtful and suspicious.

We have now arrived at the point where it is
necessary to describe the movements of Nizám
Alí Khán and the Mahrattas. The chief of Hydurabád selected the town of Pangul for his fixed
encampment, and despatched his Amírs to conquer
the Sultán's territory, and accordingly Mullik Eesau,
Khán Meeran, Yar Jung, with his division of troops
marched, and after the labours of some months,
took the forts of Gunjee Kota, Tar Puttri, Tar
Meeri, &c., and Háfiz Furíd uddín Khán, entitled
Moyud ud Dowla, with a large force marched towards Gooti, and Kotub uddín Khán Dowlat Zai,
the Foujdár of that district with his body of troops

opposed him; on the first day, however, fortune did not befriend him, and he was obliged to retreat. The second day he formed up his men in front of the enemy and displayed great courage, but at that very time he was ordered to attend the Sultán, and, therefore, he marched with his troops to Se- ringaputtun. Háfiz, when he saw it was beyond the power of his followers to take the Hill Fort of Fyze Hissar, otherwise Gooti, levelled every thing in that district with the dust, and then returned and encamped at Kirpa, and after a short time, with little trouble took the town of Kirpa, and the fort of Sadhoot, and next with four thousand horse and five thousand foot, and eight or nine guns, he commenced the siege of Gooram Konda, and occu- pied himself day and night in endeavours to take the fort, but although he made several assaults and forwarded lying letters to (persons of) the garrison, still, the commanders of the hill and lower forts did not allow doubt or fear to enter their minds, but with different kinds of fire arms (shells, rockets, &c.) and the constant discharge of cannon and musketry, they blackened the face of the courage of their adversaries.

The Chiefs of the Mahrattas, during this time having taken leave of the Paishwa, proceeded to take possession of the forts of the Mysore territory

contiguous to their frontier, and accordingly Purusram, the Chief of Mirch, took some forts and towns
in his neighbourhood : — some by force and some
by intimidation and capitulation, and annexed them
to his own district. Budruzzumán Khán the
Sáhib Soubah of the fort of Dharwar, having
strengthened that fort by the collection of stores of
provisions, arms, and ammunition, was besieged,
and for eight or nine months did justice to his
station (the Killadári) and his courage, but when
his ammunition and provisions began to fail, he
being without resource, made a regular capitulation and surrendering the fort to his enemies, he
was made prisoner by the Mahrattas, with two
thousand men; * — he, however, with his party
was confined in one place, but at length his base
enemy (the Paishwa) from the wickedness of his
disposition, ordered his servants to put the Khán
in irons, and send him to Poona; when the Khán
heard of these orders he recited the Lahowl * on the
violated faith of the agreements made by these
scoundrels, and giving up all hope of preserving
his life, he bravely with his companions retired

---

* A detachment of British troops, under Colonel Little, was
employed in this siege.

' The form of an exorcism used by the Mussulmans, the words
being لا حول و لا قوّة الا بالله

fighting as he went towards Nuggur.° The·Mah-
rattas in the meantime, in number like·ants and
locusts, crowded round his party and attacked them
on all sides with musket and sword, and notwithstanding all the brave soldiers of the Sultán could
do in their defence, they were overpowered, and
after destroying thousands of the infidels, the Khán
being wounded, was made prisoner, and he was
put in irons, and confined on the Hill of Nurgoonda,
and his followers were all trodden under the hoofs
of the Mahratta horse. The whole of the towns and
villages of that part of the country, therefore fell
into the possession of the soldiers of the Mahratta
army. Hurri Punt Phurkia, also, after taking possession of different parts of the country, advancing
by the route of Hurpun Hulli, placed a man
named Shoom Shunker, the Poligar of that district,
(who was in attendance on him as an Omeidwar,
or volunteer,) on the Musnud of his hereditary
possessions. He next reduced the Souba of Sura
under his authority. The Chief of Mirch Purusram, after having captured and garrisoned the forts
of Dharwar, Angola, Murjan, Sanore, &c. marched
to Chituldroog, and sending the terms of capitulation to Dowlut Khán, (the Killadár) engaged if he

* It does not appear from this, that he was in confinement as
before stated.

would join him and give up the fort, that no injury
should be done to him or his property, and that
a jageer of four lakhs of rupees should be conferred on him : — this faithful servant, however,
being then occupied in planning how he should
destroy his enemies, affected to accept these conditions, and in reply sent word that at night he
himself would visit the Mahratta, and in his presence make the necessary arrangements according
to his wishes. Purusram was delighted with this
answer and remained in expectation of the visit.
When night arrived, however, the Sultán's faithful
servant with two risalas of the Assud Illahees
and one thousand irregular foot, quitting the fort
with a determination to penetrate to Purusram's
tent and there do the best he could, marched into
their camp.

When he had arrived in the centre of the camp,
one of the soldiers being drunk fired off his musket,
but, although, Dowlat Khán in the first burst of
his anger ordered him to be put to death ; still,
the report of the musket roused the whole of the
Mahrattas and they got themselves in readiness to
receive their enemy. Dowlat Khán now, therefore, stretched forth the arm of courage, and with
his keen sword, cut and slashed the garment of
life off the bravest of the Hindoo soldiers, and

prostrated multitudes of them on the field of death,
and at length the whole of the enemy's troops
were scattered and dispersed, and they with their
officers took the road to Sura, and the brave
Dowlat Khán by his enterprize and valour thus
conquered his enemies, and with all the baggage
of their army, the tents, arms, accoutrements and
some horses with saddles and trappings returned
victorious to his quarters.   The chief of Mirch
now marched from Sura and arrived at Mudgiri,
and appointed a certain Mahdoo, his sister's son
to take the fort of Mudgiri, while he himself with
supplies of provisions and cattle marched to join
the English army,—during this time the Commander-in-Chief of the English, in the space of
fifteen or twenty days, having put his army in
order, (restored their materiel,) marched towards
Seringaputtun by the route of Burdi and Chen
Puttun, but the infantry of the Commander-in-
Chief of the Sultán's army who were posted in
ambush in the forest of Makri, during the dark
nights gained many signal advantages over the
army of the enemy, and every night captured five
or six hundred Bunjaras, (men who carry corn
about for sale,) with their bullocks laden with corn,
and returned after cutting off the noses and ears
of the men, and whoever brought in a nose, re-

ceived a hoon or a pagoda (as a reward,) any one
who brought in an ear, received a purtab (or half
a pagoda,) for every bullock with his load, five
rupees; and for every horse two hoons were
given :— Every day, therefore, the Kuzzaks attacked the enemy in front and in rear, and exceedingly harassed and distressed their soldiers,
often threw the followers into confusion, and
almost all their bullocks laden with grain and
stores were driven off and taken by them, and to
that height was this harassing warfare carried on,
that when the English army arrived in the neighbourhood of Kurri Khet, (or as it is usually written
Karighat,) there were no provisions or stores left
in that army. It happened also that this was the
rainy season and the water of the River Kauveri
rushed down its bed with the greatest violence,—
before the arrival of the English army, however,
the Sultán had raised four or five batteries in front
to oppose their passage and had armed them with
musketry and guns, and the brave Sipahdárs according to orders with their men, took up their
stations in each to defend them.

This was no sooner done than the Commander-in-
Chief of the English (Lord Cornwallis) before daybreak in the morning advanced and attacked the batteries, and took two of them in the most gallant man-

ner. General Meadows also with a large body of troops made a fierce assault on the Hill of Karíghat. The Sipahdár commanding there, however, whose name was Syud Humíd, poured forth from the top of the hill such vollies of musketry and such a fire from his guns, that from the shock, the assailants were completely scattered and notwithstanding the exertions they made to take the hill, obtained no advantage, and after the destruction of thousands of their men they were obliged to retire :—at this period two regiments of Europeans marched to attack the encampment of Hussein Khán Khulíl Sipahdár, which was pitched between the hill and the fort (of Seringaputtun). The brave Hussein Khán kept up a heavy fire from his guns until they arrived near, when he left his guns in the rear and formed line in front of the enemy, planting his feet firmly on the ground of his honour and duty, and in fighting and repelling his enemies he nobly distinguished himself : — *Verses*, — " Behold on each side men keen for the fight,"—" their talons sharp for bloodshed."—" With the blood spilled, so much life passed into the earth," (from the bodies of the slain) " that the earth itself received life."—" On both sides the battle was long sustained,"—" the knots of contention were not unravelled." In short with the fiery musket, the

bayonet, spear, and sword, he did justice to his
courage and character, and the Khán Khulíl
being wounded was at length taken prisoner by
the enemy.

His men also, with the pride and devotion of Islám,
after fighting bravely, one after another drank the
cup of martyrdom. But to return ; — for fifteen or
twenty days the Commander-in-Chief of the English
army was sedulously occupied in watering the river
bed of his labour,[1] and schemed and devised number-
less modes of taking the Fort of Seringaputtun, but
it was all in vain, and he became more and more
involved in difficulties, and to increase them still
further, ensued the total want of provisions, the
cries of famine, arising from all parts of his camp ;
and in addition, to the total deficiency of wood
and forage, a seer (a measure weighing a little more
than a pound) of rice, was sold nominally at the
price of four rupees, but no one ever saw a grain,
and three rupees was the price of a seer of flour
of Khush Khushí-Soórk'h, that is Raggee, (a small
grain growing in the south of India). The price
of a seer of clarified butter was eight rupees, and
a hoon was also paid for a chicken, but even at
that price they were not procurable. The Europeans could not support this scarcity of food, and

[1] Uselessly I suppose from what follows.

therefore, according to the orders of their officers the gun bullocks were killed and their flesh served to sustain their strength for some time,—when, however, the Commander-in-Chief saw the signs of impending ruin in his army, and heard of the plunder of a large convoy coming from Mala- bar under a strong escort and which was cap- tured by the Kuzzaks of Gházi Khán Bede, and the Sillahdárs of Syud Sáhib; the escort put to the sword, and the stores, &c. all converted to the service of the Sultán; he fell into deep thought and reflection, and after the assembly and sanction of a council of war, he determined to take care of himself and his army, and to that end buried all his guns in the earth, and burned their carriages, and next shot all his weak or useless horses, and then marched on his return by the route of Kurri Koort.

The Sultán when he became aware of this move- ment, determined to pass a joke on the Com- mander-in-Chief, and therefore, despatched five or six benghis or baskets of fruit under the escort of a party of rocket men, addressed to the Governor- General's[7] Persian Secretary:—some of the officers of the English army understanding the joke, or the inference to be drawn therefrom, sent the fruit bearers back with a present and an answer to the

7 That is to the Commander-in-Chief.

effect that their Persian writer was not then present with the army. In short the Commander-
in-Chief marched with the greatest difficulty, and
the light guns which were indispensable to the
army, were dragged along the road by the soldiers,
and every day from day-light to the evening, they
marched only about four miles, and although at
witnessing the miserable state of their army, some
of the Sultán's faithful Amírs and Kháns represented to him that this was the time to attack
them, and that if he would give orders they would
pursue the English army, and cast the stone of
dispersion and defeat among them, and by their
prowess bring them with their hands and feet
bound before him; still, his foresight and intelligence did not perceive any advantages in sepa-
rating his brave army from himself, and, therefore,
he would not consent to it. The Sipahsalar of
the English, therefore, moved on gently without
molestation or fear towards Ootridroog, the
Killadár of which hill fort, seeing the multitudes of
troops brought against him, suffered his courage
to ooze out at his fingers' ends, and with the keys
of the fort went to meet the Commander-in-Chief,
who received him with great favour, and found a
large quantity of stores and a great number of
cattle there, of which having taken possession, he

gave some relief to his suffering army. In fact three goats might be purchased for one rupee in their bazaar, and the famished people of his camp, being unable to support the pangs of hunger oppressing them, subsisted entirely on the flesh of goats and bullocks, and this diet gave them a flux or dysentery, and many died ; — they could not, however, obtain any kind of grain, — the Sipahsalar, or General, therefore, after encamping there two days and procuring some bullocks to draw his guns, marched towards Sondah Kupeh, where he arrived after a month's march, * (a mistake here apparently) and where Purusram joined him with stores and provisions, and the English army was relieved by him from the miseries of famine, for the Mahratta sent his own Bunjaras to the English camp, and they opening their stores of grain by his orders, in one day caused such a change in the state of affairs, that two seers of rice were sold to all for one rupee, and four or five seers of jowar * for the same amount, and consequently half the scarcity was removed when Colonel Read, who had arrived at Bangalore with an immense supply of stores and provisions, despatched thence abundance of grain of all kinds, carts of arrack and bread, with fowls,

* See Thornton, Vol. II. p. 434,
* A kind of grain grown in India.

ducks, geese, sheep and cattle, and for this he was highly complimented by the Commander-in-Chief, who in reward for his good and faithful service, appointed him to the collectorship of the revenue at Bangalore, Huskote, Kolar, Moorwakul and Hussoor, with the political agency of the Poligars of that part of the country.

The Commander-in-Chief after this, commissioned and despatched several officers with strong bodies of troops to take the forts of Makri Droog, and Nundi Gurh, and in· consequence Colonel Gowdie with three battalions of native infantry and one regiment of Europeans, besieged Nundi Gurh and battered it on all sides. Colonel Read also marched from Kolar with six hundred Sipahees to attack the same fort, and he doubtless used the utmost exertion in its capture, for notwithstanding he received a musket ball in his thigh, he took it in eighteen days. On the night of the assault, however, General Meadows went down to the trenches or breaching battery and promised the Europeans that all the plunder they took should be free; and likewise all the women who fell into their hands,—(for by the mis-management of Lootf Alí Beg, the Bukhshi there, a great number of men and women were allowed to be shut up in the fort), the General then gave orders for the

assault. The storming party immediately moved
off, and at one attack mounted and covered the
hill, and took the fort, and fearlessly possessed
themselves of the property and women of the
garrison, — thousands of women, therefore, were
violated,[b] some of them to preserve their virtue
and religion threw themselves from the top of the
hill down a precipice to the bottom, and thus
sacrificed their lives to preserve their honour. The
Bukhshi before mentioned and Sultán Khán, the
Killadár of the fort, were made prisoners.   The
fort of Makri Droog was also taken by capitulation
after a siege of three days.

[b] A gross exaggeration I do not doubt.

CHAPTER XVI.

An account of the arrival of Sikundur Jah and Foulad Jung the son of Nizám Alí Khán with Mushír ul Moolk, and a large army from the vicinity of Pankul in the camp of the English Commander-in-Chief, and the defeat of the troops besieging Mudgiri by the eldest son of Tipú, Prince Futteh Hydur; also, the death of Hafiz Furíd uddín Khán, styled Moyud ud dowla who was slain in the vicinity of Gurum Koonda — the advance also, a second time of the Commander-in-Chief of the English army to Seringaputtun, the arrival of the Mahratta Chief with his army, and the conclusion of peace between the English and the Sultán according to the views or instructions of the two confederates, (the Mahrattas and the Nizám) with other events of the year 1207, Hijri. — A. D. 1792.

AFTER the return of the English Sipahsalar (Lord Cornwallis) unsuccessful from Seringaputtun, the Sultán with his usual prudence and foresight, as soon as the River Kauveri became fordable, despatched his eldest son Prince Futteh Hydur[c] with a large body of troops, and pay for one year, to the besieged garrison of Gurum Koonda, who had to that period manfully resisted their

---

[c] In all the MSS. he is called in the heading of the Chapter the youngest son, and in the Chapter itself the eldest son, — by a mistake I suppose.

enemies. As soon, therefore, as the prince received his orders from the Sultán, he marched by the route of Turri Gira towards the Souba of Sura, and keeping his troops under cover of the jungles or forests of Gulwari and Bookaputtun, encamped his troops there, while he himself, with a small detachment (that is the Jánbáz horse) selected from the whole army and taking with him the money, marched lightly equipped towards Gurum Koonda. Hafiz Furíd uddín, the commander of the besieging party, being aware of Futteh Hydur's advance, prepared for action and left his batteries to meet him, when all at once the brave young prince with his Jánbáz horse, fell in with and charged him so vigorously and effectually, that after but little fighting he separated the head of Hafiz from his body and it was stuck on a spear's head, and the whole of his followers, being totally defeated and dispersed, fled to Kirpa. The troops manning the batteries and the trenches now abandoning their property, with their lives only, took the road to the desert of annihilation.

The conquering prince, therefore, took possession of the baggage of the defeated party, with their tents and standards, and sent them into the fort,—he next burned the materials of the batteries, and then having made over the money for

the payment of the garrison to the commanding
officer in the fort, and exhorted him to defend himself strenuously, took his receipt and marched towards the fort of Mudgiri. Sekundur Jah and
Mushír (ul Moolk) with twenty-five thousand
horse and thirty thousand foot had about this time
encamped at Moorsun Pilly and Ulumbari, which
towns are about sixteen or seventeen kose from
Gurum Koonda, but on hearing this intelligence,
being in some alarm, they sought the cover of the
hills and jungle of Sankul Pala. The brave prince,
therefore, marched by night from his encampment
to attack the besiegers of Mudgiri, who were Mahratta troops, and on his arrival there, raised the
confusion of the day of judgment among them,
and cutting off the head of the Mahratta officer
who commanded there, returned victorious to the
presence.

At this time also, Kumruddín Khán was commissioned to collect grain, cattle and other ne-
cessaries, and was sent to Nuggur. After the lapse
of about a week, the Hydurabád or Moghul chiefs,
with their army marching by the route of Bangalore, joined the English Commander-in Chief, at
or near Khán-Khán-Hulli. During this time also,
General Meadows after the capture of the hill fort
of Nundi Gurh, with a strong force marched to-

wards the Barh Mahl district, with an intention to
take the fort of Kishingiri, and assaulting the town
at night, captured it, and gave it up to plunder.
The troops then ascending the mountain, reached
the gate of the fort, when the garrison being aroused,
came forward to repel them, and crowding to the
walls poured forth such a fire of guns, musketry,
rockets and shells that they put them to flight,
and not satisfied with that, courageously pursued
them and put the greater part to the sword. The
General, therefore, marched back and joined the
grand army. Colonel Gowdie, with his division of
troops after the capture of Nundi Gurh, marching
by the route of Bangalore and Hussoor, first subdued the hearts of the Killadárs of Rai Kote with
but little trouble, and by shewing them a sum of
money and firing a few shots at the fort, it was
surrendered, and having left a garrison in it he returned. But to proceed,—as soon as the rainy
season was over, the Sipahsalar (Lord Cornwallis)
with the army of the Nizám of Hydurabád again
marched to attempt the capture of the City of
Seringaputtun, and by long stages by the route of
Chinaputtun and Ootridroog arrived there, and encamped near Kurri Gooreh one day, and then
leaving the Hydurabád army in the rear and placing
some infantry in charge of the small fort of Kurri

Gooreh, the General passed through the defile of the hills of Hurroor and still moving on at midnight fell on the batteries, which by the treachery of the Sultán's imbecile ministers had been left without defenders, and took possession of them and keeping up a heavy cannonade advanced towards the Sultán's camp. The Sultán, who with his army had encamped on this side of the river (Kauveri), and whose spies, scouts, and intelligencers had given him no information of the advance of the enemy, was completely deceived and as he had no time or opportunity to oppose them, ordered his musketeers and archers to file off to the rear, and retire to the city and place it in the best order of defence, while he himself mounted his horse and with a few faithful servants turned his face to the field of battle. From the darkness of the night, however, the troops fell into disorder and not being able to distinguish friend from foe, fought among themselves.

In this confusion Imán Khán and Mír Muhammad, Sipahdárs, with their regiments arrested the advance of the enemy and performed their duty right manfully, and to the extent of their means drove the dark vapours of pride out of the heads of their opponents, but they were at length both slain.

During this time, General Meadows with the greatest gallantry advanced, and at one assault took possession of the walls of the city, or rather suburb of Ganjam, and the Lal Baugh, which were defended by a deep ditch and strong towers. The loss of these by the neglect of Mehdi Khán, the Sáhib Dewán, left a great chasm in the foundations of the kingdom, for it happened on that night that the whole of the garrison of the fort above-mentioned, without the orders of the Sultán, were sent for under pretence of distributing their pay, and stationed before the gate of the fort of Seringaputtun, and the walls and towers being left entirely bare of defenders, the General was victorious.

As soon as this intelligence reached the Sultán, he, with the whole of his army, retired into the city, and appointed two Risalás, or regiments of Assud Illáhi Infantry,[4] (himself asking or entreating their aid) to recover the batteries which had been taken that night by the English.

As soon, therefore, as the morning dawned, these regiments marched to attack the batteries and advanced to the foot of the ramparts. It happened, however, that the Sipahsalar of the English army, was himself present in the battery, and his men consequently remained firm and drove back the

[4] The Lions of God.

storming party, and although they repeated their
assaults again and again, victory refused to shew
them her lovely face, and most of the Jánbáz,* or
bravest men sacrificed their lives in these unavailing
attacks.

The Sultán's troops (the Assud Illáhis), therefore, returned to the city. The valiant Sultán, now
strengthened all sides of the fort of Seringaputtun
with guns, mortars and every description of fire-
arms, and stationed his brave troops in all parts of
the works, and with exceeding confidence and a
truly royal spirit gave orders that his tents and
canopies made of European velvet, the silks of
Khotun and China, and the embroidered or bro-
caded cloth of Constantinople, should be raised on
every one of the towers of Seringaputtun, and the
most beautiul Bayaderes, or dancing women, and
the best singers,ᵖ and musicians being assembled
were employed day and night in dancing, singing,
and all kinds of pleasure and merriment. The
whole of the cavalry was sent towards Mysore, and
two days after this Purusram and Hurri Punt, with
their troops arrived and encamped in the neighbourhood of Char Kooli and Foulad Jung, and

* The Jánbáz, are men who devote themselves, or care nothing
for their lives.

کلارنتان ᵖ

Mushír, also with their army encamped on the
Mooti Talaub or great Tank.

No sooner did it become evident to all present,
that the siege was likely to be protracted to a great
length, and the war not likely to be easily brought
to a close, except by the sacrifice of multitudes of
lives, the fortitude and courage of the Sultán being
well known to all, than the three confederated
powers each separately in his own place sought the
means of making peace. The Sipahsalar of the
English army, in the meantime, raised a battery
south of the fort, on the side of Gunjam, and
another to the east of the fort on this side the
river, and held all in readiness for the attack. At
this period, however, the Sultán also unwilling to
continue at enmity and war with the three powerful states, by the advice, or at the instance of some
of his wise and faithful servants, despatched Vakeels
or ambassadors to the English Commander-in-chief
and to the Mahrattas, with valuable presents, and
they shaking the chain of friendship and union[f]
fulfilled their office, and made known their commission. The Sipahsalar (Lord Cornwallis) was
delighted with the friendly propositions of the Sul-

[f] Alluding to the fable of the Golden Chain, suspended before
the Gate of Anoushirwan, the just, and which was shaken, whenever any one had to complain of injustice.

tán, and determined to accept them. General
Meadows was, however, of a different opinion, and
did not give them a willing ear, and, after much
dispute and contention, he received permission from
the Commander-in-chief to attack the battery at
Somar-Peeth, which might indeed be called the
nose of the fort of Seringaputtun, and of which
the intrepid Syud Ghuffar the Sipahdár, had charge.
He accordingly attacked it, and that brave man,
Syud Ghuffar, planting his feet firmly in the field
of manhood, immediately grappled with his adversaries ; — for he advanced and met them in the
field, and with the sword, musket, and bayonet,
so vigorously repulsed them, that he drove the ball
of victory before him with the Chowkan [f] of valour,
and the storming party not having power to stand
against him retired.

After about two hours, however, while the Sultan's troops were occupied in cooking their dinners,
and had discharged all fear of their enemies from
their minds, the brave English, finding an opportunity
again, all at once made a furious assault, and with
but little trouble dispersed the Sultán's troops and
took possession of the place. [h]   This was, however,
no sooner known, than Syud Humíd and Fazíl

[f] A kind of cricket bat, or golf.
[h] He calls it the place, but means the battery.

Khán, Sipahdárs, with their troops, arrived to the aid of the defeated Sipahdár (Syud Ghuffar) and together attacking the battery vigorously, they by main force retook it, and again occupied their station in it; — but by this time two thousand English soldiers had measured their length on the field of blood, and those who escaped the sword returned to their army. On this day, General Meadows on returning to his tent, loaded a pistol and fired it off on himself: — the ball, however, did not wound him mortally, but passed through the skin of his abdomen, and he had taken up another pistol (to put an end to himself), when Colonel Malcolm, the Adjutant-General, hearing the report, rushed into the tent, seized the pistol and despatched an account of what had happened to the Commander-in-Chief. Lord Cornwallis immediately visited the General in his tent, and taking him by the hand, returned thanks to God, that he was safe, and after consoling and comforting him with kind words said, — " at this precise period, peace is our best policy, for although taking the fort and making the Sultán a prisoner be easy, and allowing both the Sultán and fort fell into our hands, still, I am not satisfied respecting our confederates, who are sharers with us in all things; for in such a case what good will result to the Company's Government ?[1] — Indeed, after mature reflection, I am convinced this is the proper time to make peace," and the General now agreed to the truth of these words.

But to proceed, — by the council and unanimous opinion of these confederated powers, the terms of agreement were arranged on the following basis, viz. — that the Sultán should cede territory to the amount of three krores of rupees and pay a similar amount in money; — that until the payment of the aforesaid money, one of the gates of Seringaputtun should be given up and remain in charge of the English troops, or otherwise, that the Sultán should send certain of his sons, as hostages for the satisfaction of the three confederated powers, to the Sipahsalar of the English army. The prudent and clear sighted Sultán, seeing the affairs of his kingdom ruined by the villany and neglect of his ungrateful and traitorous Amírs and Chiefs, of necessity was obliged to accept these terms, and the countries of the Barh Mahl, Suleem Atoorantgiri, Sankli Droog, Dindigul, Kalikote, &c., were surrendered to the English ; and the whole of the districts of Kirpa, Tar Puttri, Tar Muri, and Bullari, were given up to Nizám Alí Khán, and all the

[1] He, perhaps, does not mean this interrogatively, but affirmatively, that his proposition was the best for the interests of the Company.

country on the other side of the river Tungbhudra,
was consigned to the Mahrattas, and one krore of
rupees in money, with presents and dresses of
honour was sent out to the confederates, and agreeably to the request of the English Commander-in-
Chief, Mazuddín Sultán and Abd ul Khalik Sultán,
the sons of the Sultán, under the guardianship[k]
of Gholaum Alí Khán, and Muhammud Ruza
Khutíb, Arkati, were appointed embassadors,
(hostages) and sent off to the General, and these
wise and learned envoys, by fair and specious
speeches and words of apology, cleared the royal
road of friendship and peace from the dirt and
rubbish of suspicion and enmity, and, having pleased
the confederates with presents and offerings, caused
their removal from the city of Seringaputtun.

The confederated Chiefs having, therefore, divided the before-mentioned sum of money between
them, returned to their own countries. The
Commander-in-Chief of the English army, also,
with his princely embassadors, soon arrived at
Madras, his attention and kindness to them continually increasing, and Colonel Doveton was appointed Mír Samani, that is, to conduct their
household affairs and provide them with whatever
might be required; (this office in Persian is called

اتاليقي [k]

Mahmandari; it is here Mír Samani), and he entertained them with the respect and attention due to their rank. The English infantry now, therefore, were withdrawn from all parts, depending on the Sirkar Khodádád, and marched to take possession of the Barh Mahl, &c.; — and proclamations of peace were made in all regions.

When the Sipahsalar before mentioned arrived at Madras, a palace in the fort was cleared for the reception of the embassadors, and they were lodged there, and all necessary things prepared for their accommodation; and their friends, servants, and teachers, had permission to go and come as they pleased, particularly Muhammud Khán Surajuddowla, (who had often written to the world-conquering Sultán, desiring to make peace with him, and join him), in this matter, (attention to the princes) was most earnest and persevering, and in kindness and courtesy, treated the princely embassadors of the Sultán with more respect than he did his own children, and was continually sending them dainties for the table, fruit of the rarest kinds, &c.

CHAPTER XVII.

An account of the march of the Sultán's troops to punish the
refractory Poligars of the frontier, and of the internal regulation
of the kingdom and departments, which had fallen into disorder
and decay; also, the rebuilding or reconstruction of the Fort of
Seringaputtun, events of the year 1207, Hijri.—A.D. 1792.

From the day that the three confederated chiefs
returned successful to their own countries, the
Sultán used his utmost endeavours to understand
rightly the condition of his kingdom, and to ascertain the loyalty, and disloyalty of his chief civil and
military servants, bankers, &c., and he, therefore,
demanded from each of his collectors, Foujdárs,
&c., an account of their receipts and disbursements,
and from the context and connexion of these re-
ports he became well informed, and assured that
Mehdi Khán, his chief minister, in concert with
several bankers of the Karnatic and other traitors,
had placed his steps in the path of disloyalty and
treason, and had desired that the fame and honour
of his master and benefactor should be thrown to
the winds of peculation and plunder, and that of
this, the disordered condition of the finances and

different departments of the State was an evident
proof; as for instance, during the heat of an engagement, several guns by the direction of these
villains had their muzzles stopped up with sand or
clay. Accordingly, one by one, these wretches
received the punishment due to their crimes.
Their houses were plundered and the money obtained from them was forwarded to the embassadors to pay the instalments of the amount demanded by the confederates. The displaced Amír,
however, that is to say Sadik,[1] the false and
faithless, was restored to the Musnud of the Dewáni, or to the office of Secretary of State.—
" Ah! the wolf was entrusted with the care of the
sheep," — that old wolf, therefore, whose heart,
from the time at which he had been removed from
office, was filled with the vapours of rancour and
malice, seizing on this opportunity, accused most
of the most faithful Amírs and Kháns of neglect
and disaffection, and by arguments without reason,
and proof without foundation, (as he well knew
that as long as the Sultán had faithful servants his
evil purposes and intentions could not be accomplished,) turned the Sultán's mind against them
and in conformity to his orders they were put to
death.

[1] A play on the word Sadik, which signifies true.

During this period, certain asofs, and spies, reported to the Sultán, that to the northward of
Seringaputtun, from every corner and every bush,
rebels and robbers raised the head of pride and
insolence, and had advanced the foot of rebellion
towards the conquest of towns depending on Mysore, and without cause or consideration had bound
up their loins to injure and distress God's people,
the subjects of that state :—as for instance, one
of the chiefs of the infidels, named Vinkuti Kooreh,
had strengthened the hill fort of Kooreh Bundah,
and as is customary gave himself out as one of the
children of the Poligar of Murkeisi, and had seized
and held possession of the fort of Mudgiri, and
also, that of Ruttun Giri, and that he was in readiness to defend himself. About this time also,
Muhammud Khán the Asof of Chituldroog, and
Dowlat Khán the Foujdár of that place, despatched
an urzee (a letter) to the presence, representing
that a strange man, whom some said was a connexion or relation of the Poligar Chiefs of Hurpunhully, had made himself known by the name of
Buspa Náík, a man who had been formerly put to
death,—that he gave himself the airs of a chief of
rank, and had collected four thousand foot of the
Bedur tribe, and had strengthened Hochungi Droog
and the fort of Kootoor, depending on the Souba

of Hurpunhully and sought aid from all quarters, (even as the writer of these lines has detailed in the Tuzkirut ul Bilad wul Ahkám in the eighth Ourung or Chapter.)

But to proceed;—at this the fire of the Sultán's wrath flamed violently, and Syud Sáhib was appointed with a large force to punish the chiefs of the infidels in the vicinity of Goori Bundah, Mudgiri, &c. and Kumr uddín Khán was also despatched with a large division of troops to chastise the infidel of Hurpunhully.

The Khán had no sooner received his appointment from the Sultán than he departed, and by forced marches reached and surrounded the fort above mentioned, and with his guns and musketry threw the stone of defeat and dispersion among the garrison, and having stormed the fort took it by force of arms, and placing a detachment in that small fort marched towards Hochungi Droog. The chief before mentioned (Buspa Náík) with two thousand Bedurs (mountaineers apparently) was ready to meet him, having filled the hill fort with arms, ammunition and provisions, and indeed he exerted himself strenuously in repelling the attacks of the Sultán's troops.

For seven months, therefore, he maintained his ground and opposed them valiantly, at length,

Q

however, the Khán's anger being much excited by
the brave and obstinate defence of the infidels, he
ordered his troops to assault the fort, himself
mounting his horse to direct the attack, and his
victorious soldiers without giving any attention to
the numbers of their enemies, (they were only two
thousand he says a little before) advanced steadily
to take revenge on them, and with the greatest
intrepidity mounted the ramparts and towers, and
soon sounded their trumpets and beat their drums
in token of victory. The infidels also, advanced
to meet them like men devoting themselves to
death, and fought with such intrepidity that the
Khán himself was wounded. But at length the
besieged could no longer resist the blood-drinking
swords of the Ghazies and they were dispersed in
the desert of defeat,^{m} and the infidel chief with
four hundred men was taken prisoner. Shoom
Shunkur the nephew of the slain Náík, Buspa,
who by the assistance of the Mahrattas had seized
a portion of the dependencies of Hurpunhully, and
resided at Narayen Gir, hearing this news fled to
the other or Mahratta side of the River Tungbhudra. The Khán, therefore, according to the
orders of the Sultán for the sake of example, cut
off the hands and feet of some of the prisoners,

ادبار ^{m}

and the virile members of others and then let them go. The walls of the mountain and fort, &c. which had been the aid and refuge of the rebel infidels were razed to the foundations and he then returned. Bubur Jung, the Soubadár of that Souba, (Hurpunhully) who in the defection and contention of the troops had sought refuge in Chitul-droog, after the disturbances were quelled returned to that country, and with his own troops recovered the towns of Anigoonda, and Kunukgiri, and having sent assurances of safety to Hurri Náík, the Poligar of Kunukgiri, invited him to meet him, and on his arrival gave him the Sunnud sanctioning his continuance in the Government of that Talooka, with an honorary dress, and an elephant, and thereby gained his heart; for the Poligar, now having his mind at ease, professed himself one of the slaves or rather servants of the Sultán, and became tributary and obedient.

Syud Sáhib in the course of two or three months, after some opposition recovered Goori Bundah, Mudgiri, and Ruttun Giri, from the hands of the rebels and, having cut off the noses and ears of some of the abject infidels, returned.

Syud Humíd, the Sipahdár, from his faithful and good services was thus honoured by the present of kettle drums, an elephant and howda, and also

ennobled by the title of Nawáb, and he was then
appointed to the Government of Nuggur.

In a very short time, however, his fortune declined,
for he was taken sick and departed to the mansions
of eternity. About this period also, the wife of the
Sultán who on the arrival of the Allied Powers at
Seringaputtun, by the concussion and shock of the
battering guns[n] was seized with a palpitation of the
heart, her delicate frame being much shaken, in a
few days departed to enjoy the gardens of Paradise,
(the age of Mohi uddín Sultán being then five or
six years,) the daughter of Syud Sáhib, therefore,
according to the desire of the Queen Mother, the
young lady being approved by the Sultán, was
now selected to supply her place and was accordingly affianced to him.

It is not to be omitted here, that Kumr uddín
Khán in the hope of obtaining in marriage the
bright star of the constellation of royalty; that is
to say, the sister of Futteh Hydur Sultán, had
frequently in every service in which he had been
engaged, nobly perilled his life, but as he was not
a man of that rank or character to qualify him for
such an honour, the Sultán united him in marriage
with one of the daughters of the Nayut, (name
not mentioned) and he Kumr uddín Khán being

خفقان [n]

on all accounts hopeless, now became careless and indifferent in all matters of duty, and more than that, he secretly adopted the language of those chiefs envious of the prosperity of the Sultán, and was anxiously desiring and waiting the downfal of the State. But to return; — in a very short time by the exertions of the Sultán's troops the heads of the rebels of that quarter were brought low, and some of the Poligars, when they saw and were convinced that opposition to the Sultán was like voluntarily placing the foot of ill luck into the net of destruction, being ashamed of their misconduct, apologised and asked forgiveness, and became tributary and obedient. The Poligar of Punganoor, through the mediation of the English Commander-in-Chief, by the payment of a lakh of rupees yearly, as horse-shoe money, obtained the sunnuds or grants of his own Talooka from the Sultán, and was allowed to remain in peace.

From this period the Sultán renouncing all punishment, such as beating, flogging, or displacing the officers of his Government; after much deliberation determined on exacting an oath from each of them, and, therefore, in the month of Zi Huj, the Asofs of the Talookas and Purgunas with the Governors and accountants were assembled in presence of the Sultán, and after prayers and reading the Khotba of the Eediddoha, all of them before the mimbur, or reading desk of the Mosque, each having the Korán on his head, took an oath that he would not fail in his duty to the Government, nor make any false charge nor embezzle the money collected and forwarded by him on account of the revenue; that he would not allow the poor or the peasantry to be oppressed in word or deed,— also, that they should pass their time in prayer, their regular and daily duties, and abstain from forbidden things. After the imposition of these oaths and engagements, every one received the presents given on dismissal; but notwithstanding all this, these faithless men after taking the oath as soon as they arrived at their own Purgunas, discharged all care of it from their minds, and committed crimes the bare mention of which must be avoided, and whatever unlawful things their wicked minds conceived or desired, those they accomplished.

Ah! these fools did not know to what degradation and misery the evil influence of these wicked actions, after breaking their oaths would reduce them : — God protect us from the like. As the Sultán had a great aversion to Brahmuns, Hindus and other tribes, he did not consider any but the people of Islám his friends, and, therefore, on all

accounts his chief object was to promote and provide for them. He accordingly selected a number
of Mussulmans who could scarcely read and write,
and appointed them Mirzas of the treasury departments and placed one over each of the other
accountants, to the end that the accounts might
be submitted by them to him in the Persian language, and in the extent of his Dominions in every
Purguna by his orders was placed an Asof,[o] and in
the towns yielding a revenue of five[p] thousand
hoons or pagodas one Amil, (or collector) one
Serishtadár, one Ameen, and one Mujmoodár; all
Mussulmans, but, although the Sultán's plans involved the displacement and ruin of the Brahmuns,
such as the ·Desemookh,[q] Desepondeh and the
Kanoongo, and all of that tribe were at once thrown
out of office,—still, these people by sycophancy
and their knowledge of business, and by intriguing
with the Amils and Asofs were continued in their
employment in revenue affairs as usual, without the
knowledge of the Sultán, and the Asofs and Amils,
relying on the ability of these Brahmuns in revenue arrangements, abandoned the duties of their
offices and without fear or apprehension gave them-

[o] Meaning in other words a Foujdár or Magistrate.
[p] In some copies ten thousand.
[q] Officers employed in the collection of the revenue.

selves up to pleasure, and passed their days and
nights in witnessing dances and singing, and enjoying themselves in all ways, and the rapacious
Brahmuns' in the mean time plundered all the
Talookas at their discretion, giving half to the Asofs
while they retained the other half for their private
use. Although the Sultán heard all this from without (from his spies, I suppose), yet still keeping in
view the oaths of these faithless men, he neither
punished the offenders nor did he manifest anger
at their misconduct.

The Sultán also built a Musjid in every town,
and appointed a Muezzin, a Moula and a Kazi to
each, and promoted the education and learning of
the Mussulmans to the utmost of his power. He
himself also spent his time in prayer, reading the
Korán and counting the beads of his rosary:— as
in a Kasideh written in his praise, some one said,
" Even as he gained the stars and the heavens by
the help or the blessing of his rosary." " So by
his sword, he conquered the world and the people
of the world." The man, however, who neglected
his appointed prayers and the adulterer, he considered his personal enemies. When, therefore,
for the sake of his religion, the Sultán withheld his
hand from the duties of government, and conquest,

بی حلتی '

and ceased to inquire into the actions and conduct
of his agents and servants, every one in his place
did as he pleased fearlessly, and without restraint.
The old Kháns and faithful servants of the state
were now cast down from confidence and power,
and low men, and men without abilities were raised
to high offices and dignities: men of rank, also,
who had always been employed in the highest
duties and services, were reduced to the lowest
and humblest offices, for this reason, that it was
the wish of the Sultán that every Mussulman
should derive benefit, or reap all advantages from
his kindness alone, in order that the lower classes
of people should not despair of obtaining rank
and office.* From this cause, however, it was
that disorder and disaffection forced their way into
the very foundations of the state, and at once the
nobles and Kháns being alarmed and suspicious,
became the instigators of treachery and rebellion;
and the before-mentioned Amír (Mír Sádik), covered with kingly benefits, opened wide the doors
of deceit and fraud on the highest and lowest servants of the state, until at length the reins of the
government and the supreme direction of affairs,
all fell into his hands, and his duties and rank rose

* Or, that the people of Islám should derive all benefits and
and advantages from the table of the Sultán's beneficence alone.

higher and higher; — pride, however, now found
its way into his empty head, and most of the ques-
tions relative to government and revenue he took
into his own hands, and decided on them without
asking the consent or pleasure of the Sultán.   He
also by his oppression and violence filled all parts
of the kingdom with tumult and sedition, and regulated matters of the highest importance at his
mere fancy and caprice; — he also, by reading
charms, incantations, and by prayers for domina-
tion ' (for his necromancers burned half a maund
of black pepper every day)," he so subjected the
mind of the Sultán, that when he heard complaints
against this villain from the mouths of his Amírs,
he listened to them, but extinguishing the fire of his
royal anger with the pure water of clemency and forbearance, he did not in any way discountenance or
punish him, but on the contrary, still strove to raise
him to the highest dignities, and threw the mantle
of mercy and kindness over his crimes.   The Mír,
therefore, by the Sultán's daily increasing favour,
gained authority and power over all the forts and
castles of Mysore, and treating the chief men of

و بعملیات عزیمة خوانی و دعوت تسخیرات '

* I do not know the precise use or intention of this, but the
people of India burn black pepper as a charm to drive away evil
spirits.

the kingdom with neglect and insolence, he allowed no one any share in the conduct or administration of public affairs; — he also, dispatched misplaced or unnecessary firmáns and orders to the different dependencies of the state, — and neglected to report to the Sultán the state of the different departments, the condition of the people, and the occurrences in the kingdom.

When some of the Sultán's faithful officers saw this state of things they withdrew their tongues and hands from his service; but, to proceed, the Sultán now determined to rebuild the fort of Seringaputtun, after a new plan, and threw down the old walls and built towards the river two stone walls of great strength, with a deep ditch, towers, and curtain; — and to the south, four or five strong walls, so that the Durya Bagh, became included in the fourth fort. To the west also, he laid the foundations of four walls, or ramparts, of which two very strongly built were finished.

CHAPTER XVIII.

An account of the return of the Illustrious Embassadors (the Sultán's sons) in the year 1208, Hijri, and the naming of the Kutcheries, or Brigades of Infantry, after the great and glorious names; [x] — also, the distinction and honours conferred on the Sultán's Amírs, by the title of Mír Mírán. The preparation or formation of the throne of the kingdom, and the arrival of one of the Princes of Eeraun, or Persia, the cause of his coming being the enmity of the Amírs and Chief personages at his (Father's) court. — An account also, of the marriage of the Sultán, and a detail of the events or occurrences in the kingdom, from the beginning of 1208, to the year 1212, Hijri. — A. D. 1793-1797.

AFTER the embassador princes had remained at Cheenaputtun or Madras a year and some months, and on both sides, that is, both on the part of the Sultán and British Government, the conditions of peace and friendship had been fully established and the amount agreed on, paid, they returned, and the Sultán then made a hunting and pleasure excursion to the environs of Dewun Hully, and there on an extensive plain he received the embassadors, his sons, and their enlightened tutors or guardians, and now entertained hopes of victory and success. Gholám Alí Khán and Alí Ruza Khutíb, however,

اسما حسني [x]

from suspicion of disaffection, were placed in arrest, and the escort of the princes was dismissed with honours and royal presents.

A banquet was also given by the Sultán, at which every thing which could promote festivity and joy was provided, and every one of the Sultán's Amírs, and his brave officers received his favours with increase of rank and pay. — *Verses*, — " He increased their rank and dignity." — " His soldiers were delighted with his liberality." — " They were all well pleased and satisfied :" — " and from the weight of his favours and benefits they were all bent down to the earth." It was also in this expedition that the most distinguished of his officers were honoured with the title of Mír Mírán, and the Kutcheries [7] (brigades, or divisions) were named or numbered after the Ismá il Hussena, the names of the most high, which are ninety-nine in number ; as, for instance, the Iláhi Kutcheri was named the Rehman Kutcheri ; the Ghuffar Kutcheri, the Ghuffoor, and so on, and the Sultán having made this new regulation, returned to his capital and appointed three or four thousand Sipahees to each Kutcheri, and abolished the name of Jysh, [1] calling them all Uskur. [1] It is not to be omitted here,

---

[7] These according to Kirkpatrick, each contained several Kushoons or brigades.

[1] These words are synonimous.

that Syud Ghuffar, the faithful servant of the Sultán, was the first person distinguished by the title
of Mír Mírán, and Muhammad Ruza, the son of
Ibrahim Sáhib, the maternal uncle of the deceased
Nawáb and the grandfather of Tipú Sultán,* also,
raised the standard of Mír Mírán, and was also
styled the Binky Nawáb. The cause of his being
so named, was this ; — on some former occasion,
the Sultán had deputed him with a body of troops
to quell disturbances raised by certain rebel Naímars,
and by his bravery and good conduct, he having
brought the signs of the last day on these misguided people, and having taken many of them
prisoners, he shut them with their wives and children up in a house, and burned them alive (with
the fire of example, or as a warning to others).
He was, therefore, called by this name.ᵇ Khán
Jehán Khán, and Poornia, the Brahmun, and some
other persons of the Nayut tribe, and some the sons
of religious men, who neither possessed courage
nor a knowledge of the military art, but who were

* The following is in parenthesis, but I have thought it best to
put it in a note.—The eldest son of the said Ibrahim, that is, the
eldest brother of Muhammad Ruza, who was called Amín Sáhib,
and who was the Bukhshi of the whole of the Silladár horse, was
killed in full Kutcheri, for some trifling offence, by a Sipahi,
named Syud Mírán.

ᵇ Which in the Canarese language, means the Burning Nawáb.

acceptable to the Sultán; the patron of all Mussulmans, were raised to the rank of Mír Mírán,
and dignified by being allowed the use of kettle
drums, &c.

To the whole of the Mír Míráns were also presented dresses of gold embroidery, and tassels, with
jewels arranged in a certain order, and jewelled
gorgets. About this time the Sultán changed the
names of the different arms (fire arms), as for instance, a bundook, or matchlock, was called To-
fung; a tope, or cannon, Duruksh;[c] and a ban,
or rocket, Shuhab, &c.[d] The throne of the kingdom was also at a fortunate period finished as was
desired, but as according to the customs of the
kings of Delhi, first introduced by Sultán Julal
uddín Muhammad Akbur; for they previously demanded the daughters of the family of Juswunt,[e]
(that is, I conclude, the daughters of the Rajpoot
Princes of Hindostan), previous to the Sultán's as-
cension, a certain ceremony remained unperformed,
the Sultán having despatched hundreds of thousands of pounds to the Raja of Kutch; by his presents and favours made him obedient and willing to

---

[c] Persian, lightning.   [d] Arabic, a falling, or shooting star.
[e] Juswunt signifies possessed of courage or enterprize, but
there is some fault in the MSS. here, the word Dolee, or Dukhtur
being omitted, as persons acquainted with the customs of Hindostan will perceive.

send his daughter to him in marriage. At that period, however, fortune being employed in endeavours to ruin those professing the true religion, and the defender of God's people ; this happy result was not attained. About this time the Prince of Eeraun, on account of the opposition and enmity of Aka Baba, an eunuch (of his father's court), was obliged to quit his own country, and after suffering many hardships, arrived at Seringaputtun.

The liberal Sultán visited him, and lodged him in the suburb of Gunjam, and treated him with princely courtesy and kindness, and besides rich dresses, carpets, &c. other necessary articles, such as provisons, &c. allowed him two thousand rupees a month for the payment of his servants. As the Sultán's aim was to join and act in concert with the kings of Islám, for this reason and from friendship and good intention, he despatched embassadors with valuable presents, elephants and friendly letters to Zumán Sháh, the son of Timour Sháh, the son of Ahmud Sháh Doorrani, the Chief of Kabul and Sultán of the Ser Abdalli tribe, to propose and arrange the modes of affording each other aid and assistance, and that powerful sovereign accorded all the re-- quests of the Sultán, and honoured the envoys with many presents of great value. When the terms of peace and amity were confirmed between the two

Kings by oaths and treaties, the embassadors returned to the Sultán with rarities and presents of that country, and letters in reply, signifying the establishment of friendship and the laying of the strong foundations of amity between the two states. After some time had been passed in pleasure in the year 1210, Hijri,[f] the Sultán espoused a lady, previously betrothed to him, who was entitled Khodija i Zumán, or the Lady of the Age, (the daughter of Syud Sáhib), and the marriage banquets and entertainments were prepared, and for a certain number of days the Kháns and Amírs, who were appointed to the office of Mír Sámáni, (a kind of stewardship) arranged all things conducive to pleasure and enjoyment, and all the officers and men of the army received gifts from the treasury of that fortunate prince, and from his delicious feasts, the tongue and palates of both high and low were sweetened and gratified. By his royal munificence also, the musicians and singers, or Bayaderes, with their magic glances, were placed beyond wages or want.

The kind and friendly Sultán next sat at one table with all his Amírs and soldiers, and with the greatest condescension eat his dinner of rice and

[f] A.D. 1795. — The Prophet Muhammad's first wife was named Khadija.

R

milk with them; and during the repast said that
he and they were all brethren in religion, and
that being of one tribe it was indispensable all
jealousy and enmity should be cast aside from their
minds, and that they should unite in heart and
relying on God alone, bind up their loins strongly
to make war on the infidels, with a firm determination to devote themselves to Martyrdom in the
cause. After saying this, the Sultán with his own
generous hands distributed among his officers and
soldiers honorary dresses of a red colour, and he
then again said that they must consider these red
dresses as the dresses in which they were to devote themselves in his service. Ah!—notwithstanding all this conciliation and these favours from
the Sultán, these hard hearted men, still refused to
follow the path of loyalty and good fortune.

The next year, the Sultán determined that the
marriages of the royal princes* should be solem-
nized, and orders to that effect were issued. The
Mír Sámánán or stewards of the ceremonies according to these orders, superintended the marriage of Mihi uddín Sultán with the daughter of
Muhammad Alí, otherwise called Hujoo Mean,
and the prince was introduced to the Moon of

---

* They are called princes, although one only appears to have
been married.

the Heavens of purity and virtue, and according
to the rules and customs of the royal marriages
they were placed in conjunction on the nuptial
throne.

In the course of the third year, the wife of the
Sultán gave birth to a daughter and died about
a month after, and the child soon after drank the
milk of Paradise, or died, also.

About this time, the Prince of Eeraun agreeably
to the request of the Amírs of his own country
received permission to depart, and as the Sultán
entertained a great regard for this prince, he
honoured him with many valuable presents of
money and jewels, and at parting said,— " after
you have made your arrangements regarding the
Capital of the Sultánut of Persia, it is my wish
that you and I in concert with Zumán Sháh
should endeavour to regulate and put in order,
(divide between them seemingly) the countries of
Hindostan, and the Dukhun." The prince agreed
and pledged himself to this proposition. Previous
to this, the Sáhib Dewán,[h] (one of the Devil's
children) who was styled the Mír Asof, had frequently represented to the Sultán the wickedness,
faithlessness and disloyalty of the Sect of the
Mehdivies, who are called Ahl-i-Daira, while to all

[h] Mír Sádik.

appearance they were true men and faithful servants; the Sáhib Dewán being afraid of this tribe.
The Sultán, therefore, merely to gratify him, ex-
pelled the whole of them with their women and
children from his dominions.[1]

After this, from motives of prudence and foresight, the Sultán selected ten thousand men from
the soldiers in his army, Shaíkhs and Syuds, inhabitants of Seringaputtun, Kolar, Huskote, Dewán
Hully, Souba Sura, great Balapoor and Tanjore,
and called them his Zumrai Khas, that is his own
division or body guard, the sign or object of their in-
corporation being derived from the sentence, " dur
Zumrai Ma Ghumm Nubáshud ;"[x]—that is, " in our
company sorrow shall find no entrance ;" the letter
غین being the symbol of men of foreign nations میم
to denote Moghuls and Mahrattas; نون for Nayut;
ب for Brahman ; ا for Afghan ; ش for Sheeah ; and
دال for the Ahili Daira, or Mehdivies, these, however, were not included in the Zumra or company.
The men of this division of the army now became
the most acceptable in the eyes of the Sultán, and
all confidence was implicitly placed in them, to that

[1] See the Transactions of the Bombay Literary Society for an
account of this Sect, vol. 2, page 281.

[x] در زمرۀ ما غم نباشد   This is one of the verbal refine-
ments of the Sultán, he seems latterly to have become childish in
these matters.

degree indeed, that towards the end of the Sultán's reign, this (Zoomra Goomra,[1]) infidel battalion gained complete ascendancy over all the departments of the State, and entered boldly into all the measures of Government, — as an instance of this, one of these men named Mír Nudím an inexperienced man was made Governor of the Fort of Seringaputtun, and although the Sultán placed entire dependence on this worthless body of men, still, they were outwardly obedient only, for in their hearts they were all the devoted servants of the Sáhib Dewán, for that traitor had laid a deep plan, for the ruin of his master's state and kingdom, and this plan consisted first, in breaking up or ruining the army, and the Kháns and Amírs of rank by the reduction of their pay, and by degrading them from their offices and dignities ; after this also, by sycophancy and studying the disposition or caprices of the Sultán, and by taking the most sacred oaths,—(For God preserve us not a word passed his lips but it was accompanied by solemn oaths on the Korán) he having quieted the suspicions and doubts of the Sultán as to his intentions, he drew to his side all the Huzoorián, (courtiers or servants of the Sultán) so effectually indeed that the Urz Begi (presenter of petitions,)

[1] زمره كُمره

and others among the evil councillors, the running
footmen, messengers, servants, and spies, without
the Dewán's permission and sanction, had not the
courage to make any report whatever to the Sultán,
and the letters regarding the government and revenue which arrived from different countries were
opened by the Dewán with his own hands, and
read without the knowledge of the Sultán, and
the contents being altered or erased, other words
dictated by his will and pleasure were substituted,
and then the letters were sent to the Sultán;
indeed, the dust in that part of the country (the
court) did not rise except by his breath. Praise
to God, the other Asof Mírán Hussein, was a
low fellow and a debauchee, who never followed
any path but that of pride and vanity, and who
in different districts and towns was carried in his
Pálkí on the shoulders of dancing girls as ugly as
demons to his Kutcheri or hall of audience,—and
sometimes he assembled all the Telinga Kulavunts
(dancing or singing women) without veil or garment, and he himself stripping off his clothes
joined them naked, and thus shamelessly paraded
about among them. It will be evident from this,
what kind of order and regulation in the duties
of the State could result from a man so debauched
and abandoned as he was. The other Mír Asof

was a man named Shír Khán Cholori, who was proverbially as stupid and silent as an ox. In the hands of such foolish, incompetent men, the different departments of the State were so confounded and ruined, that of the revenue of the kingdom not one eighth part ever arrived at the treasury, and the regulations and orders of the Sultán reached no part of his dominions save the Capital. Notwithstanding all this, the mild and clement Sultán endeavoured to provide for his religious people, and he considered himself fortunate when they received their stipends.

About this time Dhondajee Wágh a devoted servant of the Sultán, (an account of whom is separately given in the Tuzkirut il Belad, va ul Ahkám, in the tenth Ourung, or Chapter) being a man of great courage and enterprise with three or four hundred well mounted horse (Do uspa), roved about and plundered in the territories of the Mahrattas, Nizám Alí Khán and the Mysore. The Sultán, therefore, sent a Kowl Namah, or assurance of safety, to him and allured him by promises of increase of rank to his service. When Dhondajee, therefore, placing confidence in the word of the Sultán came with his troops and dependents to the presence, the Sáhib Dewán in his devilry and malice found out some cause of offence against him, and with every arti-

fice and pretence sought his ruin, and at length
by false charges and suggestions to that end, he
so stimulated the Sultán that having sent for him
one day under pretence of speaking to him, he was
seized at the gate of the Palace, put in irons, imprisoned and circumcised, and the honour of Islamism conferred on him, and his body of horse
was then incorporated with the Sultán's army."
Nevertheless, the favour of the Sultán towards
that worthy man still continued to increase, as
for instance, he was allowed ten fanams Sultáni a
day, which sum amounts to three rupees, and a
teacher was appointed to instruct him, (in the
Muhammadan customs and religion) but, although
after a time, a kutcheri or brigade was named
after him, and orders were issued for his release,
it was to no purpose, for the Dewán like a scor-
pion still continued to strike at him with his veno-
mous sting, making a representation to the Sultán
to the following effect — " King of the World,
find another man equally insolent, enterprising
and brave, as he (Dhondajee), and then let him
go. For it is known to all that when he was
weak and of no account, he then beat the troops of
Hydurabád, Poona, and the servants of the Sultán,

* Dhoondia Wágh was a Mahratta, not a Puthan as supposed
by some.

and, therefore, after this to make him an officer of high rank in your army and independent, is far from good policy, for with his power and rank it is possible he might raise such a disturbance as the hand of redress might not be able to quell, or remedy," the opinion of this fool was, therefore, accepted by the Sultán, and that faithful servant and well-wisher was left in prison. At first he was named Shaíkh Ahmud, but latterly at his own desire he was entitled Mullik Juhán Khán,— but to proceed, the faithless Dewán seeing his power nearly absolute, in all matters followed the dictates of his own will and caprice, as for instance, Gházi Khán, who might be said to constitute the strongest support of the Khodádád State, without the commission of any crime, but merely on suspicion of intrigue or collusion with Mushír ul Moolk (of Hydurabád), was ordered to be imprisoned, and was then subjected to very severe treatment.

During the latter part of the Sultán's reign by the advice of certain infidel or atheistical persons he used or adopted letters from the Korán of the characters of Osmán, may God be pleased with him, which are not read, and which letters from the days of the prophet Adam to the days of the seal of the prophet (Muhammad), no one of the

Kings of Arabia, or Persia, had ever dared to
and which no learned historical, or sacred w
had deemed it proper to employ.[a]

[a] I do not know what is meant by the Author here.

CHAPTER XIX.

An account of the march of an Army under the command of
General Harris, the Commander-in-Chief of the English Forces,
agreeably to the orders of Lord Mornington, Bahadúr, and according to the advice of Aboul Kasim Khán Shusteri, and Mushír ul Moolk, (the Prime Minister of the Nizám of Hydurabád),
to Seringaputtun, and the battles fought between the Sultán and
the Sipah Sirdár, or General, before mentioned, the assault and
capture of the Fort of Seringaputtun, the Martyrdom of the Pro-
tector of the World, the Sultán, and the fall of his Kingdom and
Government, all of which events occurred in the year, 1213,
Hijri. — A. D. 1798-9.

IT may be proper to observe here, that the Sultán
in certain matters frequently acted precipitately
and without thought, and in these cases would attend to no representation, even from his most
faithful servants. As an instance, at this time, he
commissioned certain envoys and dispatched one
with presents of great value, and friendly letters to
Zumán Sháh, to strengthen the foundations of
peace and amity; and, another was sent to Kutch
to bring thence the Tika;° another person was

° This word signifies an ornament or mark on the forehead used
by ladies. It also signifies the installation or inauguration to an
office, or of a Sovereign Prince ; — here apparently it signifies the

also sent with very rich presents to the Sultán of
Room, or Constantinople. About this time, also
several Frenchmen under the command of Monsieur Seepoo, or Seboo [P] arrived at the presence
from the Port of Maurice (the Mauritius) and as in
Europe, during seven years, the fire of war and
slaughter had been lighted up daily between the
English and French nations, and they had employed every scheme and artifice in the ruin and
destruction of each other; now at the arrival of
these French, and the permission given them (to
visit Seringaputtun), the horse-shoe of the English
chiefs was placed in the Fire,[q] and they fearing that
by the aid, and at the instigation of the French,
the troops of the Sultán would proceed to the attack and pillage of the towns of the Karnatic and
Hydurabád; in consultation and concert with their
friends; they formed a plan for the destruction of
the Khodádád state; and assuming the arrival of
the French as the plea and ground of their hosti-
lities, they with the advice of Mushír ul Moolk and
Mír Alum, wrote a detailed account of these occurrences to Lord Mornington Bahadúr, then residing

Daughter of the Raja, who had been affianced to the Sultán, and
whose presence was necessary, as before stated to his accession to
the throne.

[P] سيبو M. Chapuis.   [q] نعل در اتش A common simile.

in Calcutta, and he who was looking out for such
a contingency, and who was also well acquainted
with the weakness and disorganization of the departments of the Mysore state; with the greatest
promptitude and speed embarked with four thousand Sipahees on board ship, and arrived at Madras
in the month of Shabán il Moazum, and having
assembled the army there under General Harris,
Commander-in-Chief, dispatched it in advance to
the conquest of Seringaputtun. From Hydurabád
also, Colonels Roberts and Dalrymple, with four thousand of the Bunduri, or coast Sipahees, (which force
Mushír ul Moolk had sent for to attack and break
up the troops of Monsieur Peron, the Frenchman
who had succeeded Monsieur Ramon,* the friend or
servant of the Nizám of Hydurabád, and which service they had fully accomplished ;) and with them
also two thousand Bengal Sipahees, who formerly
were stationed near Hussein Sagur, agreeably to
the orders of the Commander of the army, with
their stores and guns, marched towards Madras.
Mír Alum, also, with eight thousand horse, and
Roshun Rao, with six thousand men disciplined by
the late Monsieur Ramon, marching by the route
of Pungul Ghaut, and crossing the Ghaut of Bud-

' In this part I have followed Colonel Marriott's copy of this
work.   * Raymond.

weil and Vinkut Giri joined the English army in
the vicinity of Goriatum. As soon as the army
with its stores and artillery had assembled, Lord
Mornington wrote and dispatched two or three
letters to the Sultán, requiring him to deliver up
into his hands the Frenchmen newly arrived at
his capital; to receive and retain embassadors
or residents on his part, in the fort of Seringaputtun, and also to surrender to the English the
ports on the sea coast, such as Gorial Bundur,
Mungalore, Honawur, &c. ports where ships ar-
rive. As the Sultán among these requisitions did
not accept or agree to one, and as he sent no answer to any letter, the General according to the
orders of the Lord before mentioned (Mornington),
with General Floyd, commanding the cavalry,
General Burgess, the commander of the Europeans
and other Generals, on the 2nd of the month of
Rumzan, 1213, Hijri, marched on, and by successive stages passing by Amboor Gurh, and Tripe
toor, arrived in the neighbourhood of Rai Kote.
At that time certain interested persons represented
in studied, pompous language to the Sultán, that
the English army with certain wry faced fellows
(لج, is a disease which draws the face to one side),
from Hydurabád, were advancing to throw away
their lives, but that altogether they did not amount

to more than four or five thousand, and that the
Chief of Poona had refused to join or act in concert with them.

The Sultán, therefore, at hearing this intelligence,
appointed Poornia, Mír Mírán with a large body
of troops and other Mír Míráns to punish the insolence of the invaders of his country while he
himself gave orders to assemble his Amírs, and the
remainder of his army. The Mír Mírán above mentioned having taken leave marched towards the English army. About two kose to the westward of
Rai Kote, his cavalry having the cover of the forest
attacked the English army, but in a scattered and
confused manner, and the regular regiments of
cavalry of the enemy advanced and formed their
lines for action. The Sultán's horse surrounded
this body on all sides, and after the Kuzzaki mode
vigorously attacked them.¹ The General halted
four days before the Ghaut, and on the 2nd Showal
ul Mukurrim, moved on and encamped near Ani-
kul, when the Kuzzaks, or light cavalry, charged
the advanced guard of the English and put a
considerable body of them to the sword;—but,
in place of praise and eulogy they received from
the accursed Mír Mírán, in reward nothing but
abuse and blame, he demanding of them with

¹ It does not say with what result.

oaths and imprecations, why they attacked so rashly.

It appeared, therefore, to every one, after this that the intention of their officers was to avoid fighting, and consequently they displayed no more zeal or enterprise, and more like an escort or safeguard quietly preceded and followed the troops of the enemy as they marched along. As soon as the whole of the troops and their officers and departments were assembled under the shade of the Sultán's standard, and the Sultán became fully aware of the invasion of the enemy, he marched from Seringaputtun with the whole of his Amírs and army, and pitched his tents in the plain of Chenaputtun, on the very road which his treacherous servants had pointed out for the advance of the enemy. The General, however, turned aside from that road, and according to the advice of his scouts and guides advanced to Khán Khánhully. As soon as this intelligence reached the Sultán, he expressed great anger at his spies, and made a forced march in that direction, and in the neighbourhood of Gulshunabád, otherwise called Marooli, stopped the further progress of the enemy, he being perfectly ready for action.ᵘ The troops of the enemy also advanced and formed their

* March 27, 1799.

lines for battle. — *Verses*, — " The sound of the soldiers tramp came up from the field of battle," " and fear struck the hearts of the bravest of the brave." " The dust rose so thick that the passage to the Heavens was blocked up." " The reins of safety fell from Men's hands." " The shouts and clamour of the soldiers warmed the soul." " The neck was taken in the noose of the Kumund," (a lasso, or running knot, formerly used in battle by the Persians, and other eastern nations), " when on both sides the armies were formed." " The champions began to look out for their bravest competitors." " Punishment commenced her duty of cutting off heads." " And light quitted the eyes of the world." " From the quantity of blood that flowed into the low ground," " the earth assumed the fiery colour of red brimstone." " The two armies charged and met in numbers like ants and locusts." " By their shock they threw the world into confusion."

Although from the battle of that day, it appeared evident how the war would end, still, the faithful troops of the Sultán performed many worthy and gallant actions, and fought with the artillery of the enemy hand to hand, and shoulder to shoulder, and raised the tumult of the last day among them, and some of the bravest men closing with them

s

with their muskets and pitiless swords sent many of them to eternity — the brave men of the enemy's army also, planting their feet firmly on the ground, like men devoting themselves, threw themselves bravely on the Mussulman troops. Certain also of the brave and faithful officers of the Sultán, with their regiments came forward, and manfully withstood the fearful charge and shock [x] of the English, and like lions attacking a herd of deer, or wild asses, fell upon their assailants, and broke their ranks, and scattered them like the daughters of the Bier. [y] The false Kumruddín Khán, however, when he received orders to charge the enemy with his cavalry, alas, most shamefully neglected his duty ; for having put his body of horse to a canter, he like a blind man (instead of charging the enemy), fell upon a division of the Sultán's brave troops, and put them all into disorder, and as good fortune, and prosperity, had turned their backs on the Sultán's army, and as the signs of mischance and bad fortune every day manifested themselves more and more, many of the unfortunate soldiers gave up their lives gratuitously, and the rest regularly and with slow steps retired from the field. This un-

كوه شكوه [x]

[y]. A constellation so called, this appears to refer to the gallant resistance made by Tipú's Infantry in this action.

doubtedly was all predestined and under the power and control of no one. The English army, therefore, gained the victory and were much elated.

At this time news arrived that a body of English troops from Bombay commanded by General Stuart, bringing a very large convoy of stores and provisions was advancing by the route of Koorg, straight towards Seringaputtun. The Sultán, therefore, immediately with the whole of his troops and artillery, leaving some of his chief officers to make head against the enemy (General Harris) marched off to attack that body, [*] and in one day and two nights arrived in front of them, and gave orders for the attack. The faithful Syud Ghuffar, who in bravery and loyalty had no equal, grappled [*] with the enemy on one flank, while Hussein Alí Khán, the son of Nawáb Kotubuddín Khán carried death and destruction among them on the other, raising the flames of war to the skies—the other Mír Mírán, (General officers) also, in charging and defeating the enemy used their most strenuous endeavours, and with their swords, musketry, and artillery, put the infidels to flight;—and they giving way to the necessities of the time, and having no power to withstand the shock of the Sultán's blood-drinking lions, leaving part of their baggage behind

[*] Battle of Sedaseer.   [*] اوبجهت

them, slank into the Jungle, and occupying its
outlets remained there. The troops of the Sultán,
however, still followed them, and vigorously attacking them again, strained every nerve to rout
and destroy them; — at this critical period Muhammad Ruza, Mír Mírán, having by much entreaty obtained from the presence leave to charge,
proceeded with his division like a raging lion towards the enemy, and stretching forth the arm of
valour, it went near that the whole of the enemy's
army was cut up and destroyed. The ambush of
fate, however, having girded their loins to accomplish the defeat of the Mussulmans, a musket shot
from the enemy accidentally struck the head of Muhammad Ruza, and he fell mortally wounded. His
victorious soldiers took up his corpse and carried it
to the Sultán, who directed it to be forwarded to
the capital, while he occupied himself in the defeat
and dispersion of this force; — when spies brought
intelligence that the Bombay army had retired
from further opposition, and had marched by the
route of the Jungul to Kalicote. The Sultan,
therefore, returned to Seringaputtun, where he
had scarcely arrived, when General Harris having
crossed the river by the Ford of Hosilly, and passing Sultán Peenth, encamped to the westward of
the fort, and the next day the English regiments

made an attack on several strong outworks which
covered the fort, and were occupied by the Sultán's
troops, and after a sharp contest and the slaughter
of most of their defenders took them. On the
same day, Hussein Alí Khán, the son of Nawáb
Kotubuddín Khán, a very brave man, with the
greatest gallantry threw himself into the ranks of
the enemy, and there drank of the Shurbet of
martyrdom. The English troops now according
to the orders of their commander, collected the
materials for their batteries from the gardens of
that vicinity, and one battery was thrown up to the
westward of the fort, and another to the north
west, [b] and these having been completed, they
began to batter and breach the walls, and to set fire
to the city by throwing shells into it.

The illustrious Sultán when he saw his fortunes
in this melancholy position, and that the storm at
length had burst around the walls of his capital,
with the native firmness and hardihood of his character still determined neither to quit the fort and
retire to some other place, nor offer conditions of
peace. He resigned himself, therefore, to the will
of God, and having committed the defence of the
fortification of his capital to the Zumra (or his
choice troops) he determined to fight to the last.

بايب [b]

Kumruddín Khán who was an excellent partisan
was detached with a large body of troops to cut off
the supplies and reinforcements of the English and
their confederates, and Futteh Hydur, with the
whole of the cavalry and Sillahdár horse with
Poornia the Mír Mírán and others were detached
from the Sultán, and encamped in the plain of the
Karighat; — still at times the Sultán's horse paraded round about the English army, but as their
officers gave them no orders to engage the enemy,
mortified and distressed they rubbed the hands of
sorrow on each other. In short the army of Bombay, also arrived, and encamped in the vicinity of
Bahadúr Poora. When the Ghazies of the Faith
saw they had no choice but to light up the flames of
war, they every day well armed and appointed
threw themselves on the troops of the enemy, as
the moth flies at the lamp, and is destroyed by it,
and to repel and put to flight the authors of this
tumult and disorder, they most manfully exerted
themselves. Fortune, however, was adverse to giving
aid or success to the Sultán's troops, and they lost or
neglected the proper modes of prosecuting the war
successfully: — as for instance, the case of the Mehtab Bagh; where the faithful Syud Ghuffar was
stationed, and which he long defended against the
assaults of the enemy, and after the loss of thou-

sands of lives did not allow it to fall into their hands. At length, however, the enemies of the Sultán by their advice procured him to be recalled and stationed in the fort, and another person was sent to replace him. The English troops, therefore, immediately attacked the Mehtab Bagh, and at one assault took it, and filled it with artillery and musketeers, and thence ran on their approaches towards the fort. About that time the mild and humane Sultán, sent for Monsieur Seeboo (Chapuis), the French officer, and asked him what plans or measures he could recommend? The Frenchman replied, " that his faithful servant's advice was this, that the Sultán with his cavalry, infantry, treasure, women, &c. should quit the fort and retire to Sura, or Chituldroog, and detach a body of his troops to oppose the infidels, or if he thought best he might deliver him (Monsieur Chapuis) and the rest of the French up to the English, and then an accommodation might be made between the contending parties, or if he chose he could give up the breached walls of the fort to the charge of Monsieur Lalli, for defence, without, however, allowing Lalli to be subject to the interference or controul of the Sultán's native officers." The Sultán in reply respecting the surrender of the Frenchmen, said, " if on your account,

you being strangers from a distant land, the whole
of our kingdom should be plundered and laid waste,
well and good ; but you shall not be delivered up : "
but for an answer to the remainder of Monsieur
Chapuis's excellent advice, the Sultán sought counsel
from the Dewán, and he in furtherance of his own
views and projects said, — "It must be well known
to your highness that this people (the French)
never kept faith with any one, and your highness
may be well assured, that if you give up the fort
to their care and defence, that at that very moment
it will fall into the possession of the English, for
both these people (the English and French) consider themselves originally of the same tribe, and
they are one in heart and language."

After this villain (the Dewán), by such misrepre-
sentations, had turned the mind of the Sultán from
the right path, the walls of the city being much
battered and breached, the Sultán with an intention to quit the city had his treasure, valuables,
and Zenana (Seraglio) and also all his elephants,
camels, carriages, &c. kept in readiness to move
at the shortest warning, and held a consultation
on the subject of his departure with his Amírs.
In this council Budruzzamán Khán Nayut, incon-
siderately said to the Sultán, "may it please your
highness from the circumstance of your departure

and that of the ladies, princes, treasury, &c. the courage of your faithful servants will fail, and the bonds of union in the garrison of the capital will be broken asunder." The Sultán at hearing this looked up towards the heavens, and sighing deeply said, " I am entirely resigned to the will of God, whatever it may be," and forthwith abandoned his intention of quitting the capital. The articles packed, however, still remained ready for removal in the treasury. The unfortunate Gházi Khán,° about this time was put to death in prison by the hands of the Sultán's executioners at the instigation of the same traitor (the Dewán) ; — in fact, though the walls of the fort were battered down, still, the information was withheld from the Sultán. At length, however, on the twenty-seventh of Zi Kad, from some secret source, he became acquainted with the treachery of certain of his servants, and the next morning he wrote with his own hand a list of some of their names, and having folded it up, gave it to Mír Moyinuddín, with instructions to put his orders therein contained into execution that night, (that is to put those named to death) in order to strengthen his government.

The Mír ignorant, or unaware of the tricks played by fortune, and the changeable heavens,

° The celebrated Commander of Hydur's irregular infantry and cavalry, called Bede and Pindaras.

opened this paper and perused it in full Durbar. It happened, however, while he was reading it, that a sweeper, or menial servant of the palace, who could read and write, cast his unlucky eye upon the paper and saw the name of the lying Dewán the first in the list. This ill-omened wretch, therefore, immediately reported the circumstance to him, and said this night will be your last (or the night of your burial). At hearing this intelligence, he, the Dewán [d] kept on the alert at his own quarters, and at about mid-day sent for the troops stationed in the works near the breach under pretence of distributing their pay among them, and having collected them near the Alí Musjid, remained looking out for what ill-luck might bring forth.

The Sultán on that day, which was the 28th of the month [e] (تحت الشعاع) mounted his horse, and after inspecting the breaches in the wall or defences, ordered a party of pioneers to rebuild and repair them, and having directed his gold embroidered pavilion to be raised on the walls for his reception, returned to the palace, and then retired to the hummum or bath. As the astrologers ac-

---

[d] This man evidently supposes some secret correspondence or intelligence between the Dewán Mír Sádik, and the English General, or some of his staff.   [e] Lunar month.

cording to their calculations of the stars had determined that day to be unlucky, they represented
to the Sultán, that to mid-day and for seven Ghur-
ries (or near two hours) after, was a time ex-
tremely unpropitious to him, and also, that a dark
cloud overshadowed the fort during that period; —
that it would be advisable, therefore, that the
Sultán should remain with the army until the evening,' and give alms in the name of God. This pre-
diction of the astrologers did not please the Sultán,
still, however, in respect to the charitable donations
which repel and dissipate misfortune, whether it be
earthly or heavenly, he gave orders all should be made
ready, and after he had bathed and had left the bath,
he presented an elephant with a black Jhool, or capa-
rison, and a quantity of pearls, jewels, gold, and
silver, tied up in each of the corners of the capari-
son to a Brahman, and a number of poor men and
women being assembled, rupees and cloth were
distributed among them; — the Sultán then having
ordered his dinner to be brought, ate a morsel,
and was about to take more, but he was not so fated,
for all at once the sound of weeping and wailing
reached his ears. He, therefore, inquired of those
present what was the cause of the outcry, and it

' One copy says, seven hours of the day; that is to one, or
half-past one o'clock.

was then made known to him that the faithful and
devoted Syud Ghuffar was slain. The Sultán,
therefore, immediately left off eating and washed
his hands, saying,* "we also shall soon depart," and
then mounted his horse and proceeded by the road
of the Postern on the river, which is called in the
Kinhiri language, Holi Vuddi, towards the flag or
western battery. The Sultán's enemies, however,
who were looking out for opportunities to betray
him, as soon as the worthy Syud was slain, made a
signal from the fort by holding out white hand-
kerchiefs to the English soldiers, who were assembled in the river ready for the assault, informing
them of that event, and accordingly at about twenty
minutes after mid-day, the European and other
regiments mounted the walls by the breach, and
before the Sultán's troops could be collected to
man the walls and bastions of that flank of the
works, they with but little labour took the fort.
The garrison, although they quickly came to the
rescue and the repulse of their enemies, and with
sword and musket, steadfastly resisted them, still
as on all sides so much disorder and confusion
reigned, that remedy was hopeless, they mostly
threw away their shields and dispersed and left

* These words appear to be understood as a prophetic intima-
tion of his death.

their women and wealth to the soldiers of the
enemy, covering their shameless heads with the
dust of cowardice and disgrace. It was about the
time that the Sultán's horse and followers arrived
near the flag battery, that the lying Dewán followed
in the rear and shut up the Postern before mentioned, blocking it up securely, and thereby closing
the road of safety to the pious Sultán, and then
under pretence of bringing aid, he mounted his
horse and went forth from the fort and arrived at
the third gate (of the suburb) of Gunjam, where
he desired the gate-keepers to shut the gate as soon
as he had passed through ; while, however, he was
speaking, a man came forward and began to abuse
and revile him, saying, " Thou accursed wretch,
thou hast delivered a righteous prince up to his
enemies, and art thou now saving thyself by flight ?
I will place the punishment of thy offence by thy
side ;" this man then with one cut of his sword
struck the Dewán off his horse on the ground, and
certain other persons present crowding round him
soon despatched him, and his impure body was
dragged into a place of filth and uncleanness and
left there. Mír Moyin uddín being wounded fell
into the ditch and died there. Shere Khán Mír
Asof, also, was lost in the assault and was never
after heard of, — when the Sultán, the refuge of

the world saw that the opportunity for a gallant push was lost, (some copies say lost, and some not), and that his servants had evidently betrayed him, he returned to the Postern or sally port, but notwithstanding he gave repeated orders to the guards to open the gate, no one paid the slightest attention to him; — nay, more, Mír Nudím, the Killadár himself, with a number of foot soldiers, was standing at this time on the roof of the gate, but he also abandoned his faith and allegiance, and placing his foot in the path of disloyalty (took no notice of his master).

To be concise, when the storming party firing furiously as they advanced, arrived near the Sultán, he, courageous as a lion, attacked them with the greatest bravery, and although the place [b] where he stood was very narrow and confined, he still with his matchlock and his sword killed two or three of the enemy, but at length having received several mortal wounds in the face, he drank of the cup of Martyrdom.

After this, therefore, what followed in the slaughter of the Mussulmans, the plunder of their property and the violation of their women had better be left untold. The French troops in the Sultán's service during this time wrung their hands

[b] Said to have been a gateway.

in grief, and having assembled at the gate of the
palace, they fired a few vollies at the storming party
and then desisted from further resistance. The
whole of the treasures, wealth, and property of all
kinds belonging to the Khodádád state, therefore,
which was great in amount beyond conception, fell
into the plundering hands of the English soldiers,
and they who had been reduced to death's door by
the want of supplies and the dearness of provisions,
who had been obliged to pay two rupees for a Seer
(a measure of little more than a pound) of rice in
the Hydurabád camp, when they could get it there;
three rupees for a leg of mutton; and two rupees
for a bundle of the roots of grass; — now all at
once became well provided and rich in all things.
The princes with all their property, the Zunana or
women of the Sultán, and Kurím Sáhib his brother
were all taken prisoners. Futteh Hydur the Mír
Lushkur or Commander-in-Chief, however, who
with the infantry, cavalry, elephants, artillery, and
stores, the strength of the kingdom, was encamped
near the Kurighat Hill, at hearing this dreadful intelligence, marched and took the road to Chenrai-
puttun.

The English officers now after great search,
having found the body of the injured and oppressed
Sultán, it was placed in a Pálkí and left for the

night in the treasury, and the next morning the whole of his children, servants, and friends having seen it for the last time and established its identity, the General gave leave for its interment, and it was deposited in the earth in the Lal Baugh, in the Mausoleum of the deceased Nawáb, on the right side of his tomb, and there rested from the treachery and malice of faithless servants and cruel enemies. Alas! this great accumulation of state and grandeur, pomp and splendour, at a single revolution of the faithless and ever changing heavens, was so lost, that no one knew what had become of it. Truly, — *Verse,* — " what garden of prosperity ever raised its head to the skies ?" — " that in the end, the cold withering blast of desolation did not tear up by the roots ?" — " Upon whose head did fortune ever place a kingly crown" — " upon whose hands and feet death (fate) did not ultimately cast its bonds." The following are elegiac verses written in commemoration of this event.

" Tipú Sultán was slain unexpectedly." " He shed his blood for the sake of the religion of the true God," on Saturday the 28th Zi Kad, " The day of judgment manifested itself," " At the seventh hour, from the morning, blood flowed from every wall and door, in the streets of Seringaputtun." " Tipú lived in honour fifty years, and reigned seventeen."

—" His heart was ever bent on religious warfare,"
" and at length he obtained the crown of martyrdom, even as he desired." " Ah! at the destruction of this prince and his kingdom." " Let the
world shed tears of blood." " For him the sun
and moon shared equally in grief. " " The heavens
were turned upside down and the earth darkened."
" When I (the poet) saw that sorrow for him per-
vaded all." " I asked grief for the year of his
death." " An angel (Hatif) replied, let us mourn
his loss with burning sighs and tears "—" For the
light of the religion of Islám has departed from the
world,"

نور اسلام دین ز دنیا رفت ¹

In short the agents of fate and destiny did what
they willed, or what was in their power. All the
elephants and camels, the treasures, jewels, valuables, and property of every description, belonging
to the Sultán, fell into the hands of the English.
The new throne was broken up, and the diamonds,
jewels, with chests full of jewelled gorgets and pearl
necklaces were sold by auction (هّراج) and all the

¹ This last verse gives the date, 1213 Hijri, or A. D. 1798-9.
Another person found the date in the words نان بیوه شکسته شد
— the bread of the widows and orphans has failed — another
او نسل حیدر شهید اکبر شد Alas! the Son of Hydur is a
Martyr.

arms and stores were plundered, and the library of
the deceased Sultán sent to Europe.

After about a week, Kumr uddín Khán, who
anxiously prayed for such a day, came with great
pleasure, to offer his services to the General commanding the army, and having negotiated with
him respecting his Jageer, Gurum Koonda, and
after receiving the Sunnud, entitling him to retain
that district, he marched thither with his drums
beating to take possession.

Futteh Hydur Sultán also, when he saw the
symptoms of fear, distress, and despair, prevailing
among his followers, and at the same time heard
the consolatory, and conciliatory language used by
the English General and other of his officers; included in which were hints or hopes held out of
his being placed on the throne; abandoned all intention of fighting or further opposition, although
several of his bravest officers, such as Mullik Jehán
Khán,[k] who after the death of the Sultán had been
released (by the British troops) and had presented
himself to the service of Futteh Hydur Sultán,
also Syud Nasir Alí Mír Mírán and other Asofs

[k] That is to say, Dhoondia the partisan chief, whose force was
so effectually dispersed and destroyed by the British troops under
the command of the Honourable Colonel Arthur Wellesley, at
Konahgul, or according to the Persian account, Kotal Behnawer.
— See Thornton's History, Vol. III. p. 93. 115, &c.

dissuaded him from peace, and strenuously urged
him to continue the war. They represented to
him that the Sultán had devoted his life only to
the will of God, but that his dominions, his strong
cities and forts were still in the possession of his
servants, and that his army with all its artillery
and stores was present. That if there were any
intention to reconquer the country, or if any spirit
or courage remained, now was the time (for exertion), and that they were ready and willing to
devote their lives to his service. This descendant
of Hydur, however, notwithstanding his constitu-
tional or hereditary bravery, at the suggestion of
Poornia, the Brahmun (who in promoting the
ruin and destruction of the Khodádád state had
employed his utmost endeavours) and the advice
also of other traitors of the Sultán's court, (every
one of whom thinking of his wife and family, abandoned his duty and loyalty,) was deceived, and
acted in conformity to their wishes, at once rejected the prayers of his well wishers, and consequently washing his hands of kingly power and
dominion, he proceeded to meet and confer with
General Harris.

After this was arranged, according to the advice
and desire of the (Governor-General) council, a
boy of five years of age, one of the lineal descen-

dants of the former Rajahs of Mysore, was seated
nominally on the Musnud of his hereditary claim
to that territory in Mysore; and a country, the revenue of which amounted to thirty lakhs of pagodas,[1] was assigned to him under the prime ministry
or guardianship of Poornia, and all the children and
relations of the deceased Sultán, (many of whose
ladies remained,) with Kurím Sáhib and his family
were sent to Rai Vellore, and a liberal salary was
allowed to each of the princes, and to the present
time they still reside in the fort of Vellore.

The following is the list of the princes,—
Mohí uddín Sultán; Hydur Alí Sultán, known
by the name of Futteh Hydur, this is the eldest
of all the brethren; Abdul Khálik Sultán; Moiz
uddín Sultán; Subhán Sáhib Sultán; Shúkur
ulláh Sultán; Gholám Ahmud Sultán; Gholám
Muhammad Sultán; Surwur uddín Sultán and
Yasin Sáhib Sultán; with his two brothers, Jama
uddín Sultán;[m] and Monír uddín Sultán. These
with their women, families and followers, all reside
together.

The mind of the General (Harris) being now
perfectly at ease, he proceeded to Chitul Droog,

[1] 3,000,000.
[m] This prince was residing in London two or three years ago,
but died lately at Paris.

and took possession of all the hill forts and strong-
holds in that part of the country; and placing
garrisons in some of them, he returned to Madras,
and thence sailed for Europe, accompanied by
Colonel Read, General Floyd, &c.

The countries of Gootti, Rutna Giri, Murkeisi,
Hurpun Hulli, Ani Goondi, Punookoond, Murg-
sura and other places were added to the territo-
tories of the Nizám of Hydurabád for a time.
After this, however, in the year 1215, Hijri, (A.D.
1800) they were given back in Tunkhwah to the
English Government. (To defray the charges of
a subsidiary force apparently.)

Mullik Jehán Khán (Dhoondia) who had escaped
with only one horse, in a short time, by his own vigorous exertions increased in strength and reputation
so much, that he collected together a body of twenty-
five or thirty thousand horse and foot, and raised
a great tumult in the country, situate between the
Kishna and Tungbhudra Rivers, and Babur Jung,
and others joined him. By the aid also of the
chief of Kolapoor, during a sharp engagement, he
in a furious charge, killed Gokla the Mahratta and
Purusram the chief of Mirch, and having struck
off their heads stuck them on the points of spears.

At length, however, it fell to his lot to be opposed to the English troops, and after much hard

marching and fighting day and night, during which time no decisive action was fought, (although in this period his successes were great and he obtained much spoil,) still as he had no fort or stronghold in his possession to which he could retire and deposit his stores and followers, and by that means compete with the English on fair ground; after a hard struggle for two years from the treachery of the Afghans of Kirpa and Kurnole, he received such a defeat from the English troops (under the command of the Hon. Colonel Sir Arthur Wellesley) in the neighbourhood of Kotal Bhanawur,[n] (called Konahgull by Mr. Thornton) that with the exception of his name and fame, no memorial of him whatever has remained.

Kumr uddín Khán for a time exerted himself in a vain desire to obtain a government, but at length a fatal disease, too terrible to be described, seized him and he died in great agonies. Many of the Sultán's Sïrdárs or officers, however, such as Budruzzumán Khán, Gholám alí Khán the elchee or envoy; Muhammad Ruza Khutíb; certain of the Mír Mírán and Sipahdárs; the brethren of Beorhunuddín, that is the sons of Lala Meean; Gholám Alí Bukshi, Gundahchar, &c. receive liberal salaries from the English East India Company,

[n] Otherwise Hunoor.

according to their respective claims. A thousand
praises are due to their courage and constancy.*

In the year 1215, Hijri, Hydur Alí the son of
Kurím Sáhib (the son of Nawáb Hydur Alí) made
his escape from the English and joined the Mah-
·rattas.

* I think the Author here speaks ironically.

CHAPTER XX.

A description of the amiable personal qualities, the disposition, manners and usages of that ornament of the throne of silence, (death) Típú Sultán.[p] These, notwithstanding from the abundance of evidence and proof they require no detail, or amplification, still agreeably to custom, a concise account of them is here given.

In his courts the splendour of kingly magnificence and majesty were well sustained. He had profited to a considerable extent in all the sciences. He wrote and composed with ease and elegance, and indeed had a genius[q] for literary acquirement, and a great talent for business ; and, therefore, he was not obliged to rely on the aid or guidance of others in the management of public affairs. He had a pleasing address and manner, was very discriminating in his estimation of the character of men of learning, and laboured sedulously in the encouragement and instruction of the people of Islám. He had, however, a great dislike to, or rather an abhorrence of, the people of other re-

[p] See the 115 Psalm, 17 verse, for a similar expression. The Dukhmas or Sepulchres in which the Parsees deposit their dead, are called by them " Towers of Silence."

[q] سليقه

ligions. He never saluted (or returned a salute
to) any one. He held his Durbars from the morning
until midnight, and after the morning prayers, he
was used to employ some time in reading the
Korán, and he was to be seen at all times with his
Tusbíh or rosary in his hand, having performed
his ablutionary duties. He made only two meals
a day, and all his Amírs and the princes dined with
him. But from the day on which peace was made
between him and Lord Cornwallis, Buhadúr, (to the
day of his death) he abandoned[r] his bed and bed-
stead and slept or took a few hours rest on certain
pieces of a coarse kind of canvas called Khaddi,
(used for making tents) spread upon the ground.
He was accustomed on most occasions to speak
Persian, and while he was eating his dinner, two
hours were devoted by him to the perusal (from
standard historical works,) of the actions of the
Kings of Persia and Arabia, religious works, tra-
ditions and biography. He also heard appropriate
stories and anecdotes related by his courtiers. Jests
and ribaldry, however, from the repetition of which
the religion of Islám might suffer disparagement,
or injury, were never allowed in the courts or as-
semblies of that most religious prince. For the

---

[r] Apparently from having made a vow to that effect, a custom
· ery common in the East.

sake of recreation (تفنس),* as is the custom of men of high rank, he sometimes witnessed dancing (or was present at the performance of Bayaderes). He was not, however, lavish or expensive in any of his habits or amusements, not even in his dress, and contrary to his former custom he latterly avoided the use of coloured garments. On his journeys and expeditions, however, he wore a coat of cloth of gold, or of the red tiger stripe embroidered with gold. He was also accustomed to tie a white handkerchief over his turban and under his chin, and no one was allowed to tie on, or wear, a white handkerchief in that manner, except himself.

Towards the end of his reign he wore a green turban Shumlehdár, (twisted apparently) after the fashion of the Arabs, having one embroidered end pendant[t] on the side of his head. He conferred honours on all Professors of the Arts, and in the observance of his prayers, fasts and other religious duties, he was very strict, and in that respect the instructor,[u] or example of the people of Islám. Contrary to the custom of the deceased Nawáb, he the Sultán retained the hair of his eyebrows, eye-

---

* To see or patronize the skill and accomplishments of the Bayaderes.

[t] طرّ ه   [u] علام

lashes, and moustaches. His beard, however, which
was chiefly on his chin, he shaved thinking it not
becoming to him. In delicacy or modesty of
feeling he was the most particular man in the
world, so much so that from the days of his child-
hood to that of his death, no one ever saw any
part of his person except his ancle and wrist, and
even in the bath he always covered himself from
head to foot.

In the whole of the territories of the Balaghaut,
most of the Hindoo women go about with their
breasts and their heads uncovered like animals.
He, therefore, gave orders that no one of these
women should go out of her house without a robe
and a veil or covering for the head. This im-
modest custom was, therefore, abolished in that
country. In his strict sense and keen perception
of propriety and right he was unequalled. It happened that on some festival or day of rejoicing, he
went to his father's private apartments to present
his congratulations to his mother, and after the
performance of this duty, and presenting dresses
to her and her servants, he laid himself down to
sleep a short time. During this period two ladies
of the deceased Nawáb's family, both of them
young and handsome, (God knows with what intention good or bad) came forth from their apart-

ments, and began to rub his feet. While, however, they were doing this, he awoke, and when
he saw they were the widows of the late Nawáb,
(or in the place of his mother), he became exceedingly angry at their presumption, and trembling
with rage, said, " you are both of you my mothers,
what insolence is this of which you have been
guilty and by which you have blackened my
face, what answer shall I give to-morrow to my
father ?" (meaning at the day of judgement) after
this expostulation he sent for one of the Eu-
nuchs of the Serai and directed him to punish
these women, so that they might be an example to
others.

In courage and hardihood the Sultán took pre-
cedence of all his contemporaries, and in the management of a horse and the use of the spear in the
world he had no equal, as will appear after an
attentive perusal of this work. He was fond of
introducing novelty and invention in all matters,
(and in all departments) as for instance, the year
called Muhammadí, an account of which has been
before given, also the names of the solar months.
For although these months are in usage among
the Hindus, still as they became necessary in the
computation of the revenue accounts, he gave
them names from the Persian according to the

Abjud, Howuz, Hutti[x] system of numeration as
Ahmudi Bihari, Julwi, Darai, Hashimi, Wasai, Zu-
burjudi, Hyduri, Tulooi, Yuzdani, Eezudi, Bunai,
&c.

Towards the conclusion of his reign he abolished
these names[r] and called the months by others;
such as Ahmudi, Bihari, Tukki, Sumri, Jafuri,
Hyduri, Khasrovi, Deeni, Zakuri, Rahmani, Razi,
and Rubbani. In the same manner also, the
names of the cycle of sixty years, as for instance,
Ahud, Ahmud, Ab, Ja, Bab, Buja, Abud, Jad,
Jah, Ouj, &c. He also altered the impression on
the hoon, or pagoda, and rupee to a different form,
as has been before related in the account of his
coinage.

The Siduki was an ashrafi or gold mohur, with
the same impression, as the rupee.

The Farooki was a pagoda, having on one side
the name (Farooki) and on the other the letter ع.

The Imami rupee also was of the weight and
value of two rupees, this is now current.

The Bakuri, a half rupee.

The Jafuri, a quarter of a rupee.

The Kazimi, two annas.

The Fulum or Fanam was called Rahuti, and
the Anna, Ayuh.

ابجد هوز حطي [x]   طرح [r]

The terms employed in the measurement of grain were as follows. The Seer (a weight a little more than a pound) was called Duk, and weighed twenty-four fuloos or halfpence.

The Mun was called Atul, which is about four Seers or pounds.

The Dhurra which is a quarter of a Mun was called Hoob.

The Kurro which was sixteen Asar or Seers, was called Bede, and the Khundi which is twenty Kurras, Ahya.

Besides these inventions, his workmen cast guns of a very wonderful description, lion mouthed; also, muskets with two or three barrels, scissors, pen-knives, clocks, daggers called sufdura,—also, a kind of shield woven and formed so as to resist a musket ball.

Besides these he also instituted manufactories for the fabrication or imitation of the cloths of all countries, such as shawls, velvet, Kímkháb, (cloth of gold,) broad cloth (European), and he expended thousands of pounds in these undertakings.

His chief aim and object was, however, the encouragement and protection of the Muhammadan religion, and the religious maxims or rules of the Soonni sect,—and he not only himself abstained

from all forbidden practices, but he strictly pro-
hibited his servants from their commission.

He also formed regulations on every subject and
for every department depending on his government, every article of which was separately written
with his own hand. If, however, he dismissed
any one from his office for any fault, or neglect,
he after correction and punishment, was accustomed to re-appoint him to the same office again;
and from this cause it was that during his reign,
treachery gained head so far as to cast his kingdom and power gratuitously to the winds.

On the top of his furmáns or public papers, he
was accustomed to write the words,—" In the
name of God" — in the Toghra character in his own
hand, and at the end his signature was in this
form so

THE CONCLUSION OF THIS WORK.

PRAISE and Thanksgiving to God.* — (*Verse*) —
" that what I asked has been granted by him."
When the commands obeyed by the world,
brilliant as the light of the sun, exalted as the
Heavens, of that great personage (the name of this
great personage is not given, it being in the
opinion of the author sufficiently known) whose
heart is the abode of purity and sincerity, were
issued to this gatherer of crumbs from the table of
the wise and learned, that he should reduce to
writing in a plain easy style the History of the
Kingdom of Mysore, and with his pen describe faithfully the whole of the wars and conquests, (made by
the rulers of that country) ; notwithstanding certain
contingencies and worldly troubles (عوايق), * and
the scanty means and mean abilities of this ruined
man ; the difficulties which beset him in obtaining

الحمد لله و المنّه *

* Some variation in the MS. here. I have followed Colonel
Marriot's copy.

the means of subsistence and the fatigue of a long
journey; all strongly operated to prevent his attempting so great an undertaking and threw the
stone of indecision at the glass of the firmness of
his determination; and his mind the finder or
inventor of signs, or symbols,[b] with the tongue
of humility in detailing such high and praise-
worthy qualities and actions, said "what power
has a speechless ant that he should be able to
move a mountain ? or what strength has a fly that
he should take such a burden on his shoulders ?"
being, still, however, obedient to the commands and
bound to the orders of the great personage before mentioned, without attempting the difficult task
of composing flowery and ornamented periods, a
few lines have been written describing the conquests
and other events of the reign (of Tipú Sultán), his
excellent qualities and singularly good disposition.
Stories of his liberality, the relation of occurrences
displaying his kind and forgiving temper, his generosity to his friends, his zeal for the propagation of the religion of Islám, and for the destruction of infidels and infidelity. In writing these
details the purity of the author's pearl-stringing
pen, has not been sullied by the dirt of misrepre-
sentation or falsehood, such being the practice of

خاطرنكته ياب رموافزين [b]

U

hired sycophants of low character, or of foolish rhapsodical writers only. (The Author after using the third person, now speaks in the first—but, to continue as he began). The hope and trust of the Author, therefore, from the princely sons and dependants of the Sultán is, that they will look on his book with the eyes of impartiality and approbation, and give him the meed of praise in proportion to his claims and merits, which (meed) is the harvest of the life, and the chief source of gratification and delight to the poor and needy scholar. And as the History of the Nawáb Hydur Alí Khán Bahadúr, and a commentary on the reign and actions of Tipú Sultán, are both included in this work, for that reason the Author has sought and found the year of its completion in the word (تواریخ) Towárikh (which is the plural of تاریخ [c] a date of a month or year, and a term generally applied to history,) that is to say, it was the year 1217, Hijri. (A.D. 1802) ; and it was on the 9th of the month of Rujub ul Morujub, that he turned the reins of the horse-like pen from his career on the race-course of the paper to the end, that his soul might be released from the toils of anxiety, hard study, and deep reflection, and that at

[c] From the root ارخ signifying the time of making or composing any thing, as a Book, &c.

length the object of his desires (rest, or the completion of the work) might shew him her lovely face

من هنا أشرع في المقصود برب الموجود

From this commences the accomplishment of the Author's desires, by the aid of the Lord of all existence.

PRINTED BY W. NICOL, 60, PALL MALL.

Lightning Source UK Ltd.
Milton Keynes UK
06 September 2010

159489UK00008B/42/A